AM I SAFE YET?

STORIES OF WOMEN
SEEKING ASYLUM IN BRITAIN

ACKNOWLEDGEMENTS

As women asylum seekers, we have always been made to feel worthless, forgotten and isolated. Together as Women Asylum Seekers Together (WAST) we have had the courage and strength to speak out. We refuse to be silenced. WAST has a growing network of support from many individuals and organizations. The making of this book is a remarkable achievement which evolved from our determination (and that of our supporters) that our fight against injustices, our pain and suffering will not be in vain and that we will be heard, understood and will inspire others to speak out.

We would like to thank sincerely our volunteer supporters Ursula Sharma and Hannah Berry, who interviewed and recorded us on a dictaphone and then transcribed and edited our stories. Without their time, patience and support this book would not have happened.

Many other people gave their time to the production of the book. These include Jane Lawson, who advised on the book layout and overall design. Zarrin Shannon designed the cover and the chapter motif. Nikki Harrison took the photographs. Sarah Irving copy-edited the final version and Vicky Marsh kept everyone on track throughout the process. Hermione McEwen of the Greater Manchester Immigration Aid Unit gave valuable advice on chapter seven.

Special thanks are also due to Natasha Walters for her support and contribution to the book, and Nelly Mann for her advice. Finally thanks also to Jackie Ould and Emma Britain of Ahmed Iqbal Ullah Education Trust for valuable editorial advice and support throughout the production process.

Our WAST group was awarded a grant of £10,000 by Awards For All (the Lottery grant scheme for local communities) and a grant of £1,000 from Manchester City Council (as part of International Women's Day) towards the production and launch of the book. These were welcome funds which are gratefully acknowledged.

CONTENTS

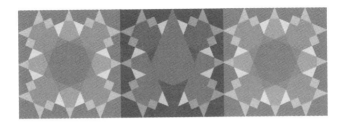

FOREWORD

By Natasha Walter

I first met Farhat Khan when she was speaking at a meeting in the House of Commons at the beginning of 2006. It was an unforgettable experience. I was by then aware of the injustices suffered by refugee women in the UK, but I had never before met a woman who could explain with such passion and yet such calm the repercussions of these injustices on her own life and the lives of others.

Farhat Khan explained to the audience how she had fled from her home country, Pakistan, in order to escape from the oppression of her husband and his family. He objected to her independence and had taken his anger out on her physically for years. But the crunch point had come when his family had got Farhat's two young daughters engaged, effectively forcing child marriage onto them. She could not bear to think that her daughters would share her fate, and she decided to escape to a country where, she believed, women's rights were given respect. As Farhat told of the abuse she suffered before she and her daughters came to this country, the audience was moved to tears.

When Farhat got to the UK, however, she found her fight was not over. She was refused asylum and fought for six years before that decision was overturned and she was finally given leave to remain here. During that long struggle for security she became the most effective advocate of this urgent cause: that women's experiences of what is called gender-related persecution - which includes rape, so-called honour crimes, threats of female genital mutilation, trafficking for forced prostitution - should be taken seriously by decision-makers in the UK asylum process. In the speech that Farhat made when I first met her, she rightly drew attention not just to her own struggle, but to the fact that at the moment the government is failing in its responsibilities to many women.

Our government currently pays lip service to the idea that women who have experienced serious persecution at home and whose own government refuses to protect them from further abuse should be able to seek refuge in our country, in the same way that victims of persecution on the grounds of race and religion and ethnic background can seek asylum. But in practice women who have fled such persecution are too often turned down for asylum here. Often decision-makers do not believe their stories, and even where they are believed, their experiences are often seen as not fitting them for protection under refugee law. This is true both of women such as Farhat Khan, who have experienced persecution in the domestic context, and for women who have undergone persecution by state agents such as police or soldiers.

I can't help thinking here of a woman I met only the week before writing this, who had been raped and beaten up on more than one occasion by police in her home country, Azerbaijan, for being a Christian. Her asylum determination stated that while it was "unfortunate" that the police had "exceeded their authority" this did not constitute persecution that was sufficiently serious to fit her for refugee status here. This is not an isolated case, any more than Farhat's situation was particularly unusual. Women are coming here out of desperation, having fled the grimmest kinds of violence, and we are refusing to recognise them as refugees. This means that they can then be made destitute, they are liable to prolonged detention, and they can be forced on to aeroplanes back to the countries where they believe that their lives are in danger.

The stories of such women go almost unheard. I have worked as a feature writer and columnist for national newspapers for 15 years, and over this time I have seen how difficult it is for women refugees to be heard, even if they have the courage to speak out. Newspapers will cover stories of violence against women if they think their readers will identify with those women - if they are British women, in other words - but the tales of women who have recently arrived in this country are perhaps seen as too alien and distant to be explored with any great interest. I think this indifference partly stems from fear; fear of the social changes that might come about if we admit that we should not put up impregnable barriers between ourselves and the victims of these gross abuses. And yet, in all honesty, there are not so many asylum seekers that it would create any problems for our society if we were to treat them with dignity and justice rather than leaving them, as we currently do, to negotiate an unjust, confusing and tortuous system in which they are often set up to fail.

When I heard, soon after hearing her speak, that Farhat had set up a group of women asylum seekers who were determined to campaign for justice for their cases and to tell people about the harsh situations they live in in the UK, it seemed both extraordinary and somehow unsurprising. For too long the voices of asylum seekers themselves have been pushed to the background of these debates. I had seen how effectively Farhat had taken the platform during her own campaign. If anyone could, it was clear that she was the person who would be able to encourage other women to speak out.

And this is what the organisation she founded, Women Asylum Seekers Together, has achieved. It has given women who were once entirely silenced the resources and courage to speak clearly. As they do so, you can catch glimpses of another world, in which the rights and freedoms that most people take for granted must be fought for every step of the way. I have been privileged over the last couple of years to meet and talk personally with a number of the women whose stories are contained in this volume. Each one of them has their own story of great suffering and injustice, and also of inspiring courage. They deserve to be heard.

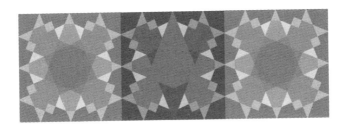

1

'WOMEN ASYLUM SEEKERS TOGETHER' AND THE MAKING OF THIS BOOK

By Farhat Khan

'Am I Safe Yet' is an attempt by a group of asylum-seeking women to give the reader an insight into the nightmare world from which they escaped and the treatment they receive in the country they come to in the hope of protection and security. These real life stories are told by members of a group called WAST, formed by asylum-seeking women themselves. The narratives can be difficult reading but there is no gentle way to describe the terrible reality that forces these women to flee from their home countries to seek international protection, and the often inhumane way in which they are treated while passing through the asylum system in the UK. Some of these stories have been told over and over again as the story-teller bares her very soul, telling intimate details to often complete strangers, in the hope that they will support her in the struggle to stay in the UK; other stories are being told publicly for the first time as the story-teller finally finds the courage within herself to share her painful experiences with others. These women relive the horror of what has happened to them each time they tell their story but they are willing to do so in the hope that it will create wider awareness about the persecution faced by women, in countries the British government declares are safe for women asylum seekers to be returned to. They also hope that in telling their stories they will begin the long and difficult process of healing the deep wounds each one of them carries on her soul.

Women Asylum Seekers Together (WAST) was established in 2005 by a group of 'failed' asylum-seeking women whose applications for asylum had come to the end of the legal process and who faced potential deportation. This group of women came from diverse backgrounds. Some had belonged to poor families back home while others came from a more privileged background; some had never been to school while others had received university education; some were hardly out of their teens while others were already grandmothers. They spoke different languages and belonged to a number of African and Asian countries. Their reasons for fleeing their countries were as varied. The list was long and bleak: ethnicity, political activity, religion, domestic violence, the threat of honour killing, forced marriage, female genital mutliation (FGM), sexual orientation, etc. But what had brought these women together was what they shared in common - the persecution they had faced in their own countries, often because they were women in societies that do not accept the rights of women; the lack of willingness or the ability of their governments and often of their own families to provide them protection; and the refusal of the Home Office and the Immigration Courts to grant them asylum.

WAST is a self-led and self-support organisation. Learning from their experiences and sharing skills and knowledge, WAST members help each other take forward their asylum applications as well as set up and run public campaigns to be given the right to stay in the UK. WAST aims to provide women asylum seekers with an environment where they can feel comfortable and where they can meet other women in a situation similar to theirs.

But even more importantly, WAST endeavours to fill some of the emptiness that each asylum-seeking woman feels in her heart, an emptiness created by loneliness and isolation, loss and rejection, despair and humiliation. To put it in the words of one WAST member, "The emptiness in my heart that I have not been able to fill all these years, the feeling of loss, the grief I have felt every day since coming here - for my country, my home, the children I have not seen all this time, my brothers and sisters, the rest of the extended family, friends, colleagues, the graves of my parents who have died while I was in the UK, the work I did while in my country - this emptiness makes me yearn every day to go back and live once again in the place which was home despite all the problems we faced there, a place where we belonged. A place where we did not have to justify our presence, constantly and apologetically, a place where we were not reminded day in and day out, overtly or covertly, that we were asylum seekers, assumed to be here for the riches and the comforts we could not have had back home, bogus, outsiders, gate-crashers, a burden on the tax payer, the lowest of the low, a place where we would have identities of our own and not just be Home Office reference numbers."

Members say that WAST is an important part of their identity. As one WAST member puts it, "WAST has given me a useful role within our community and has helped me to gain the confidence and the self-esteem that I had never had a chance to develop. The opportunity to be seen as a valuable person with skills has helped to transform me from someone with no hopes and aspirations to someone with the will and the courage to fight for myself and for others too." WAST aims to raise public awareness about issues that force women to seek asylum and the shortcomings of the UK's asylum system in dealing with the applications of asylum-seeking women. Its members regularly deliver lectures and workshops at educational institutions and are invited to speak at public events all over the country. In November 2007,

Manchester City Council awarded WAST its Elizabeth Gaskell Award for the group which had done most to "promote the role of women in public life", and for its "significant contribution to local gender equality."

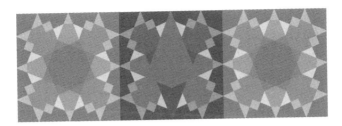

2

BREAKING GENDER NORMS

All societies have expectations as to how 'proper' women should behave, but the penalties women pay when they do not conform to these norms vary in their severity. Hummera and Victoria are seeking asylum because their refusal to obey oppressive norms has put them beyond the protection of the law and has lost them the sympathy and protection of their families. Hummera has been rejected by her family for choosing a husband without their approval; she and her husband could face charges of adultery or abduction under Pakistani law. She suffered violence at the hands of her family and her husband was threatened with death. Victoria has been punished for her sexuality by a forced marriage to a brutal cousin and the threat of female circumcision. She could also find herself on the wrong side of the law in Sierra Leone where lesbianism is prohibited.

HUMMERA

As in many countries, marriage in Pakistan is often seen as a means of making alliances between families and it is usually negotiated by the couple's elders. Parents expect to control the timing of their children's marriages and the choice of partners. A young unmarried woman would not be expected to have informal social contact with men who are not close kin, and dating is certainly not approved of. Whilst in Pakistan there is not a caste system in quite the same sense as there is in most parts of India, marriages are generally arranged between members of the same status group.

I was born in Lahore, into an average family, neither rich nor poor. I have two brothers, both younger than me. My mother was a housewife and my father worked for a transport company. From the age of three I attended an English medium school near to our home, before going on to college and then university. My father, a very strict man, did not want me to continue my education, but he reluctantly let me attend university as long as my younger brother escorted me there and back and made sure I did not associate with anyone. After university I began an M.Phil in education, a correspondence course. I was offered a lectureship because of my excellent grades, but I could not take it up even if my father had let me, because by that time I had met Aamir.

We noticed each other one day at the university, where he came to use the sports facilities. We snatched a conversation and started to like each other. We met again a few times, but before long I had left and was studying from home. Occasionally my brother would take me to the campus library, and we managed to meet secretly in a big park nearby.

At home, all decisions were referred to my father, and we were all afraid of him, so I knew I couldn't tell any of them about Aamir. I held on to the hope that when the time was right, Aamir would gain his parents' consent and that they would persuade mine that we should marry. But everything happened much sooner than I'd imagined, because my father suddenly announced that he was arranging my marriage. So I told Aamir he must ask his mother straightaway. She refused, saying that he was not established in a career and that it was his older brother and sister's turn first. There was also fact that they were Mughals and we are Ahmadi - in Pakistan people always want their children to marry within the same caste. But when my parents set my wedding date to a stranger, we became desperate. Aamir and I decided to marry, thinking that it would force our parents to accept us being together and everything would be fine. One of Aamir's professors agreed to arrange two witnesses and a Maulvi (the religious person needed for the Nikah, the Muslim marriage ceremony) and the rites were performed at his office at the university.

At first, my mother wouldn't believe me about the marriage. When she saw I was serious, she started abusing me and became... I can understand her feelings because she was very scared of my father. She told him and my brothers, who started beating me. They wanted to know who he was and where he lived. My father locked me in a room so I couldn't escape. He said we had to divorce and then they'd kill Aamir. My brothers thought divorce irrelevant; the important thing was to have Aamir dead.

When Aamir told his own family, his brother tried to kill him and he ran away. He had gone by the time the police arrived at his house, called there by my parents who had forced me to give them his name. I was in a terrible condition. They continued to beat me and accuse me every day, vowing to find and kill Aamir and then me.

A few weeks later, a woman called on the phone, asking for me. I was forbidden to speak to anyone outside the family, so my mother passed me the receiver but told me to stay silent. I listened, and there was Aamir. The telephone operator had agreed to help him contact me. He told me not to worry, that he was in Islamabad. He said, "I am arranging something and will be in touch soon. I am with you." I relaxed a bit, even though I knew my family and the police were all after him. Aamir had gone to the same professor friend, who was very clear about the danger facing us and said we must get out of the country. Through another friend, Aamir managed to contact an agent and withdraw some money. A few days later he called me, the same way as before, and told me what to do. After 11 o'clock, while my family slept, I left home. Aamir was waiting in a rickshaw; we took the train to Islamabad and stayed with his friend until all the arrangements were complete.

On the day we left Pakistan we saw ourselves in a national newspaper, as wanted criminals. It really scared me. I was also afraid in Islamabad because I knew my father had many contacts from when he worked there. His job meant he had links in every Pakistani city.

The agent travelled with us. He kept hold of all the papers and passports and said nothing about asylum, just that the UK would save our lives. He said we could choose Oxford, Birmingham or Manchester, because those cities had big communities from Pakistan and India where Aamir could find work and we'd be able to rent accommodation. We took a bus to Oxford, arriving late the same night.

We started walking in the dark, but after a while we sat down and cried like children because we had no idea where to go or what to do next. An old Pakistani gentleman saw us and asked what was wrong, and we told him everything. He took us into his home and gave us a room, and I did cleaning and stitching for the old lady. They knew a community worker, who took us to the Oxford refugee centre. That's where we discovered we had to enter a legal process to get asylum in this country. It was then that we came to know we were not allowed to work. Southall Black Sisters[1] found us a good solicitor and our case began. We were given accommodation in Manchester.

Ever since we left home we have been like blind people, being led along but never knowing where each step will lead. We have no agency, we just follow. Everything seems stuck - no work, no education, nothing. It's just us and our faith. We try to have hope.

The first house was nice and our Abdullah was born there. After our big crisis, our son brought us our first happiness. However, the area we lived in was difficult because it is an Asian area and everyone asked why we were there on our own and why we were not working. One man saw our story in the Metro News and told Aamir he was going to send it to Lahore and get his son to copy it and post it everywhere, so that our families would find out where we were. We don't know if he did it. People were not friendly. A neighbouring girl who was my age did visit me for a time with her two small daughters. But when my second son was born and she had another girl, she must have been jealous because she never spoke to me again. Then the tenancy ended and we were moved to another area.

In terms of our asylum case, it was refused. We lost the appeal but won a second appeal on human rights grounds.

1. Southall Black Sisters was established in 1979 to meet the needs of black and Asian women. It challenges abuse and violence against women and works to empower them to gain control of their lives. As well as campaigning it provides counselling and advice to women who have experienced violence or abuse.

Then the Home Office appealed that decision successfully and we ran out of options. We went to the National Coalition of Anti-Deportation Campaigns, who helped us start campaigning. We found some good friends and made useful links, especially with the National Union of Journalists, Aamir's union. Now we have a new solicitor and have some hope again, but know that the policy remains that people in our situation must relocate somewhere in Pakistan. We are trying to gather evidence to show that this is not a safe option. As I explained before, my father works in the transport business and has feelers everywhere. A young couple can't hide in Pakistani cities; you can't get work or accommodation and everyone wonders about you and asks about your family. If anyone was suspicious they could contact the police and they would come for us because of the report filed against us. Nothing has changed in Pakistan. We read in the paper that a young couple had hidden themselves in Lahore, in the next street to where I grew up. Their cousin found them and said their parents had forgiven everything, so they went back. The family killed first the boy and then the girl, then cut them up and threw their pieces in the river. That was just five days ago.

We don't know when everything will be OK, or if we'll be deported and what will happen to our kids if we are killed by our families. Before we were worried about our own lives but now we worry about our kids - God gave us two lovely kids and we don't want to lose them. Aamir heard that his father has died and that his family blames him and are even angrier than before. My husband is very co-operative and very loving and caring with me, but it is because of me that he is in this condition; because of me he has lost his golden age, his youth. He cannot work, he has put his life at risk and left everything just for me. These things are always on my mind. Sometimes I tell myself that these five years have just been a bad dream. That we'll wake up, start work and education and say, "Now we are alive again. God has given us new life."

VICTORIA

Homosexual acts are illegal in Sierra Leone. In 2004 Fanny Ann Eddy, leader of the Sierra Leone Lesbian and Gay Association, was brutally murdered by intruders who broke into her office and strangled her. She had made a submission to the UN about the homophobic harassment and violence faced by the Lesbian and Gay community in Sierra Leone.

The 1990s were a period of ongoing civil war in Sierra Leone, the primary issue being control of Sierra Leone's diamond mines. The 'rebels' to which Victoria refers are the Revolutionary United Front, who had bases in neighbouring Liberia and conducted attacks of great brutality on civilian populations.

I was born in Freetown, Sierra Leone. I was brought up as Muslim; my other name is Maryam, which is a Muslim name. We kept the fasts, but I found it hard and I was not very good at praying. My Dad was a businessman and he would go to the villages and bring palm oil and other goods to the city. He would also trade in other nearby African countries like Gambia.

I went to school and I got as far as secondary school, but in my last year at secondary school, that was the time the rebels entered Freetown, and this disrupted my education. There had been conflict before but now the rebels were actually taking over the capital. They entered the town in 1997. I had to leave school because there were no teachers in the school. The rebels were just killing people. People were afraid that the rebels might force them to join them; they might kidnap you or even kill you. If they wanted your car you just had to give them the key or they would take it by force. So everybody stayed at home when they took over the capital.

The rebels caught my Dad while he was in the village and told him to join them so that he could bring them information from the towns. But he ran away from them. He was scared that they were going to send somebody to kill him in the city. So he left my country and went to live in Denmark. He died there later.

I did manage to sit my GCSEs but that was the last time I went to school. I did not go to college, but I did do a six month course in computers. Then I looked for work but it was very difficult. It is very hard in Africa to get good jobs. Since my Dad died we could not pay for anything. My Mum had problems paying the rent and the landlord would come round and harass her. With five kids she could not manage on her own so we had to move back to my mother's family's house. By that time my auntie was really the one taking care of the house, as my grandmother was old. My mother did not have much say in the house. My auntie is a top business woman, trading with other African countries. So she was the head of the household, spending money for the food, and she really took over our family. It was only me that was working to support my Mum. My brothers and sisters are all younger than me and they were too young to be at work. Even then my pay was very irregular; sometimes they would pay me on time, sometimes not.

I got a job, but that was when my problems with my family started. At the weekends I did not have to work and I would go to the beach with some of my friends. Rumours started going round about the people I was hanging out with. You know how you tell your best friend a secret, and she will tell her own friends as well. The owner of the bar on the beach where we went was bisexual, so most lesbians and gays would go and meet there. I would usually go as it was a nice place to relax on Friday, Saturdays and Sundays. I had known that I liked women for some time, even at school I had thought this. So it was when I went to the beach that I met Emma, this lady from America. She had come on holiday, she was mixed race, but in Africa as long as your skin is light they say you are white – we don't even know what is mixed race! She had come with a friend. She had been talking about going to Australia because she liked travelling. She always said that since she was young she had intended to travel all round the world. She had been in Gambia as well as Sierra Leone. I was about nineteen at that time when I made friends with her.

Now rumours started getting back to my family that I was lesbian. My Mum was not too angry, it was my auntie that objected. You can talk to your Mum and she will listen to you, but because of our circumstances we could not afford things, so in everything she had to look up to my auntie. If something is going on in the house, we had to talk to my auntie. When she heard the rumours she said it was a disgrace for my family and she told my Mum that she should get me married. If they let me continue this life I would disgrace the family even more.

Sometimes in Africa a man who wants to marry a woman will go to her family and ask to marry her. He will bring some money and say "I want to marry your daughter." He may not even tell her, it can be arranged behind her back. I didn't know anything about it, but my auntie had chosen one of her sons for me. My auntie had had various boyfriends when she was travelling around trading, and she had three or four kids in the town by them. All of them have their own dad and were living in different places. She arranged for one of the elder sons who was doing business with her to marry me. He brought some money but I told them I don't want to get married, I just want to live my own life. They put a lot of pressure on me. My Mum was more supportive at first but because of money, because she was dependent on my auntie, she started supporting my auntie as well. My younger sister also supported me. My lesbian friends did not like what was happening to me but they were in the same position, hiding their own life from their own families.

People thought I was a bad thing. If your family hates you the neighbours will be scared to accept you because they don't want their kids to get spoilt. So when my auntie started spreading the news out I felt under pressure to agree to the wedding, even though I did not really know the boy. It was too much, everything just came at once... My husband was too rough on me, whatever he wanted to do he would do by force, even if I fought him off.

I was not happy and he was very rough with me, because his Mum was like that with me also. I went to the police to complain about him. But the police don't care; they said it was a family matter. They told me my family should sort it out. I went to the police twice when my auntie and my husband were out on business. I was thinking that they would come with me and help me leave the place and find somewhere else. I was trying to find someone in the neighbourhood who would accept me to stay but everybody was against me. They themselves started calling me names because the family was telling them not to encourage me. Anyone who would accept me, my family would turn against them. So I had nowhere I could run to. I did run away once, to an uncle who lived in the village. But my uncle would not accept me in his house, so I had to come back and face the humiliation from my cousin and family.

When they made me get married my auntie said they ought to send me to the Bondu Society. Maybe if I went there it would 'cure' me so I could stay in the marriage. The Bondu Society does female circumcision. It's a full circumcision, they just cut off everything. Even when they are using the blade they use the same blade on any number of girls. You have to have money to get the ceremony done. You have to buy a new dress for the girl and pay for a big celebration but if you don't have money you can't do that. The idea is that when the girl comes out from the circumcision she will not be too happy so they do a big celebration for her. It was the custom in my family if they could afford it, but because we did not have any money, I had not had it done.

Sometimes it is done for three year old girls, even young babies. People think that a girl should be circumcised before she gets married, it's like she is dirty or she is not a proper woman. My auntie wanted me to have it done. The mentality is, 'get married, have kids, that's what it is to be a proper woman.' Otherwise they start calling you names. There are some women in Africa who are against it now and I am happy for that, they will not be doing that for innocent girls coming up. That's why they prefer to do circumcision young. If they abolish that I will be happy because my little sisters, I don't want them to go through that. Luckily I left Sierra Leone before they could do this to me.

I had a friend, a lesbian, who lived quite a long way from where I lived. One day she came around and I explained everything to her. I told her that I had been forced to get married. I gave her the details of Emma, my American friend, and asked her to call her. Eventually I got in touch with her and said I needed some money to leave the place. At that time I was hoping that I would be able to go to Gambia but I was scared because I didn't know anyone there. Also my auntie does business in most of the African countries in the region. But I did not know where else I could go.

When she came to Africa Emma had come with a friend, a businessman. He was actually a Sierra Leonian who had lived in USA for a long time. He was still in Sierra Leone. She gave me his telephone number and I contacted him in the hotel where he was staying. She had asked him to help me get a passport and everything. The plan was that I should go to America with him, travelling as though I was his business associate. But when we came to the airport in London we had to change flights and go through transit and that was when we got separated. At that time several planes were coming at once, so there was a big crowd of people in the airport. I was looking for him everywhere in the crowd but he had my passport. When they asked me for my passport I told the woman I did not have any documents with me, that the man I came with has the passport. I did have copies which I had made in Sierra Leone, but they would not accept them. They just took me aside somewhere. I was scared and confused - so many white people, it seemed very strange. I waited for some time but the guy still did not come. He must have taken his flight to America. So the officials gave me a form to fill in and I asked the other African people there what it was. They said it was for asylum – you have to ask for it as you don't have a passport. I said I am going to USA but they said you don't have any documents. I filled out the form with the exact details as I knew they were written in my passport.

I had thought I was going to America but I lost that guy in the crowd. I still do not know why he left me like that. At the end of the day I had thought I was going to see Emma. He was not the one who had spent the money. But when they started asking me questions I did not say anything about her because I did not want to disclose her identity or anything. You see I had only known her for a month or two. It was not that I should just say everything about her. I did not know her well enough to know what she would want. Later this was to count against me because when they refused my asylum case they said my case was not credible because I could not name her.

When I was coming I was pregnant with Scott, but I did not know it. Then I started feeling sick, even in the hostel where they sent me from the airport. I thought the food did not suit me. When I knew I was pregnant I felt very bad but I did not go to the doctor because at that time I had no GP. Then the NASS[2] dispersed me to Swansea. I didn't like Swansea. "What kind of place is this where I can't see a single person in the street, and it is so cold?" I thought, "let me go back to Africa and let me face the whole situation there." At that time I was not even thinking about staying here, I just wanted to go back.

When I had been in the hostel I had met a Sierra Leonian lady. I used to go into central London to get some African food to make me feel a bit better. I went there twice and I met this woman I had known a bit in Sierra Leone. I told her about my situation and she took pity on me. She said I was welcome at her place and she gave me the address where she lived and all her contact details. When they sent me to Swansea I was so unhappy I tried to call her. I had about 40p left on me, but I put it in the phone and called her. She was a refugee also. She had run away from the war and had lost most of her family. She had been granted Exceptional Leave to Remain for four years. So she told me, "Victoria, I only have a one bedroom place and I have one child as well, but you can share with us". So I said, OK, I would manage whatever is the situation. I used to manage in Africa so I can manage here. So I left the house where they had sent me in Swansea.

When she saw me the first time she did not know I was pregnant, I did not even know myself at that time. She said I should go and see a GP. I had to wait for NASS to send document I needed to register with a GP, proof of identity etc. So eventually I went to the GP and I said that I wanted to abort. He told me I would have to go and have a scan so he sent me to the big hospital and they gave me an appointment for a month's time.

2. NASS (National Asylum Support Service) was the section of the Home Office responsible for the accommodation and support of asylum seekers until April 2007, when it was replaced by the Borders and Immigration Agency.

So when I actually went to have the scan I was already four months pregnant. The GP told me in this country we don't do abortions after three months. So I had to accept it. But I did not have any money.

I had been sleeping in a chair at my friend's place but when you are pregnant and you are sleeping like that the baby is always on one side, not in a good position. At one point they had to rush me into hospital; the midwife said that where I was staying was no good for me. So they put me in a hostel again. I was there for three weeks, and then they moved me to Rochdale. But even when I was in Rochdale I was not happy and I kept going back to London. My midwife in London told me I must see the doctor in Rochdale. So I had to stay – my belly was too big. In the end I gave birth in Rochdale. But NASS kept moving me from one place to another - five different places within six months – Rochdale, Chadderton and Manchester. I would stay in one house for a few weeks and then I would have to pack up my things and move to another place. When I tried to tell them they said you just have to move. It is inhuman and unfair to my little boy Scott because of the effect it has had on him. That is why he is having speech difficulties, even to say a few words is hard for him. But they don't care about how people live. They abolished slavery but it is the same treatment we are having, you have no choice where you go, you are put in different houses and they don't care what those houses are like as long as they can say that refugees have shelter, somewhere to sleep. The house they gave me in Oldham, the cooker was not working so I had to buy food in the street all the time. I couldn't cook for Scott, and we were cold in the night. In one house, water was pouring in when it rained. When the council came and checked the house they said it was not fit for anybody to live in.

My asylum application was refused because I wouldn't identify the woman who was my girl friend and so they did not believe me, but at that time I was scared to say anything. Now I have a campaign going and we are hoping to make a fresh claim. I hope they will accept it because I do want to stay here now. I have some friends and on Friday night when the campaign group had a benefit for me, I felt someone is looking out for me. They made me feel that I do have a family once more, somebody that will be behind me. I really appreciate that and I will try my best to show it to those who have helped me. It really made me feel happy.

3

POLITICS - AND THE POLITICS OF RAPE

In Britain rape is treated as an offence against the person, committed by one individual against another. Another way of looking at rape is to see it as an exercise of male power. At the most prosaic level it is an exercise of the physical power of a man to violate a woman (or sometimes a man) against her (or his) will.

Seen in a political light it can be regarded as an instrument of control. The stories of many asylum seekers involve tales of rape (and especially gang rape) used explicitly as a means of punishment or intimidation of women (and sometimes men as well). It may be perpetrated by agents of the state or, as in the three stories which follow, by political groups who either have the tacit support of the state or who are beyond its control. The experience of rape leaves many scars, physical and emotional, and recounting a story of rape is stressful in itself - the more so when, as in Naima's case, the Home Office response to the pain of disclosure is disbelief. The crime of rape is notoriously difficult to prove if there are no witnesses and the circumstances of the victims are often such that at the time it is difficult for them to obtain the kind of medical evidence that would convince the authorities here.

NAIMA

According to its own Gender Guidelines, the Home Office recognises that women are often subject to persecution and violence on account of their husbands' political activities. In dealing with Naima's case the Home Office claimed that Bangladesh was safe, being on their 'white list' of countries considered safe from the point of view of human rights and political persecution. Yet the Foreign and Commonwealth has this to say about Bangladesh:

Political violence has increased generally in recent years… Successive governments in Bangladesh have failed to curb serious human rights violations… these violations include torture; deaths in custody; arbitrary detention of government opponents and others; excessive use of force leading at time to extra-judicial executions; death penalty; acts of violence against women; and harassment of journalists.

Foreign and Commonwealth Office country profile on Bangladesh, updated January 2007.

In Bangladesh, as in other parts of South Asia, for a woman to be raped is a matter of shame for her and by extension for her family, especially her husband; she has lost her honour and he has been unable to protect her. The women is liable to be blamed for her rape (she must have done something to provoke it) and even where she is seen as blameless in the matter – as in the case of the thousands of Bangladeshi women raped by Pakistani military during the war of independence from Pakistan in 1971 - it may be difficult for her family to accept her back. Thus for the victim of rape to publicly claim her victimhood is to expose herself to more shame and criticism; silence may be seen as the less painful option.

I was born in Dhaka, in Bangladesh. I am one of twelve sisters; my father married twice but he never got a son. My father is dead now. He was an important man – he was chairman of the local council. He also did a lot of social work and helped many poor people. He was a rich man with a big house and he started a charity to provide food for the poor; every day he would have food cooked – chapattis, rice, meat, fish, proper meals. My mother helped him with this.

Our family lived a comfortable life. I went to school in Dhaka and studied to college level. I started a BA degree course but I didn't finish this because I got married while I was at college. My parents found my husband for me. My husband has three brothers and four sisters. He also comes from a well-off family. His father is dead now but he was an engineer. My husband had his own business, import and export. When I got married I went to live with my husband's family in another area, Bhola. It's practically an island, the sea is all around, and it's on the Bay of Bengal.

I was always interested in women's rights. Both before my marriage and afterwards when we were living in Dhaka I was involved with a group concerned with women's development and rights. I was a volunteer and would go to women's houses. We worked with uneducated poor women. We would meet once a week and discuss issues like dowry and domestic violence. We would give literacy classes so that they could write their own names and addresses and help women to improve their finances by earning money.

But I came to this country because of my husband's political activities. I myself was not involved in any political parties, but my husband was involved with the Freedom Party. This party was one of the opposition parties, opposed to the Awami League which was the ruling party for many years. The Freedom Party had groups in the cities and in the countryside and my husband was a very active member.

He had had problems because of his political activities even before our marriage but while we were in Bhola these problems got worse. He had many enemies; he was widely known to be an opposition person and was constantly being threatened. He was always very good and he tried to reassure me, but I was frightened in Bhola. I had had no idea that my married life would be like that. We wanted a peaceful life so my mother-in-law and I came back to Dhaka so people in Bhola would not know where we were.

After I returned to Dhaka, I was living in the city in a rented house where nobody knew who I was, but my husband was still in Bhola, hiding in his sister's house. But the Bhola police were after him, there were lots of problems for us. Someone must have found out who I was. I did not know how they came to know all this, but men kept coming round and asking where my husband was. I lied to them and said my husband had nothing to do with the Freedom Party. Then they started to tell me they knew I was lying and that if they found my husband they would kill him and chop him in pieces. They even threatened to kidnap my son. They kept coming round so I phoned my husband and said don't come back home, people keep coming here and they seem to know everything, so I feel it is dangerous for you to come here. I was very afraid. So he stayed away, at his sister's house. We were very alert in case anything should happen because we were getting death threats all the time.

One day some men came to our house and broke the door down. I refused to give them my husband's proper address where he was staying. They told me call your husband or bring your husband here They were putting pressure on me, but I said I don't know whereabouts he is at the moment because sometimes he goes to foreign countries on business. They said I should call him on his phone or give them his number. I said that he doesn't have a mobile. So then they looked through the flat but they couldn't find his address, so they started smashing the place up, breaking the furniture. They started shouting at me and slapping me, pulling my hair, still telling me to give my husband's address or call him. Then they tied me up and took me in their car. Really I don't know how long I was in that car, maybe one hour. Anyway they took me to a new building, still empty, a quiet place. They took me inside and started asking me again. They gave me a mobile and said call your husband, tell him you are in a relative's house and ask him to come and meet you and give this address. But my husband knew all my relatives' addresses, he knew where all of them lived, they just wanted to see if I really knew where my husband was. I totally refused to tell them. One of them was smoking and he held my hand and pushed the lighted cigarette down onto my hand, saying "Now you are going to tell us." It was very painful. I begged them to let me go. I said, "I don't know why you have taken me, I don't do politics. If my husband has done anything wrong then go to the police station, why have you kidnapped me? My child is asleep at home and what will happen if he wakes up and I am not there?" Then they started to slash my arm with a blade but still I refused.

Then they bound my mouth so that I could not shout and pulled off my sari and then I understood what was going to happen. After the third man had raped me I passed out and they dumped me somewhere near my home. The next day I found myself in hospital where some local people had taken me.

I want to forget what happened at that time but I can't forget, it always comes to my mind. People here always tell me it is not your fault. They sympathise and want to help me, but sometimes I wish people did not want to help me because to make my case I always have to speak about this, about things I am fed up with remembering. If I go back to my country people will tell my son that his Mum was raped, maybe they will tell my children my story. It is a matter of shame in my country. When I came here I thought now I am free, no one will criticize me, nobody will ask me anything, but of course when I gave the interview in the Home Office I had to tell everything. Now I have a campaign group to support me and everywhere I speak publicly in my campaign. In order to get the right to stay here I have to tell this story over again, telling all the things I want to forget. People who listen when I speak look at it one way, they may sympathise, but when I speak I feel it all over again. It happened in my life, but I am seeing it repeatedly, it's as though I were in that situation again.

After all this we decided that it was too dangerous for us to stay in Bangladesh. I had never had any intention to come to England; I never imagined that I would come here. We didn't leave our country because we wanted to come here to get work or a house. We came because we were forced to escape, because we did not want to put my family in danger. At first we decided to go to Jamaica. We did not have any real friends there, we only went there because our country has no connections with Jamaica, no embassy there. We thought no one in Bangladesh would ever have the idea of looking for us there. My husband had applied for visas to go to Japan or Singapore, but he only got a visa for Jamaica. We left in a great hurry.

We stayed in Jamaica for about six months. But there was no job and we were always scared. When I had travelled before it had just been for a holiday, not in fear. But when we arrived in Jamaica, everything was different. We were confused and we could not tell whether people were well-disposed to us or not. Also Jamaica is a violent place, every day there was fighting downtown. Wealthy tourists come to Jamaica from all over the world and we had been told that sometimes people from abroad were robbed. People would take their money and jewellery, even kill them. We had no idea whether what people were saying was true or not, but somebody told my husband this and he was very very scared. We did not feel secure and also our money was running out. We had no idea what to do. One day a friend of my husband called from America and suggested that we go somewhere and seek asylum. He said we should go anywhere where human rights are respected.

When we came to England my husband made a claim for asylum in his name only because it was his political activities that had caused us to be persecuted. But his application was turned down in 2002. In 2003 I got my second son. In 2004 the Home Office detained us and told my husband that as a failed asylum seeker he would be deported. We were interviewed separately in two different rooms. But I resisted being sent back, I told them everything about my own case, how I was also a victim. Then they released me but they kept my husband, though he got bail later. I then put in a claim to asylum in my own right (separately from my husband) while he was in detention, but this too was eventually refused. They refused to believe my account.

I am a woman and I want justice. I came to this country to seek help from the government, to find protection, but they never took my claim seriously. They told me I am a liar, they never respected me that I am a victim or believed that I had been raped. I am witness to what happened to me, but they are always saying show us your evidence. Here evidence means doctor's papers. But my doctor was threatened by the people who kidnapped me not to give any evidence to the police. The Home Office could not understand this situation. In any case what happened to me was a matter of shame. At the time I wanted to hide it. Lots of women don't report rape because they think they will face further humiliation, or even further violence. My kidnappers told me don't go to the police, don't try to do anything, next time we will not just kidnap you, we will kill you. They threatened to kidnap my son also. And in Bangladesh even if a woman reports rape, the authorities do not take it seriously.

Meanwhile in March 2005 my husband went to sign at Dallas Court[3] and they took him and they forced him to go back to my country. They deported him and separated my family. When we came to this country I did not know anything about it and my husband did everything. He is a part of my family, children need parents, their father. And I need my husband. Sex is not everything, men and women need each other's support. Why did they separate us? But I also thought, my husband's life is uncertain but at least I think I am safe. I was thinking of my children. At that time I was pregnant and my baby girl was born in 2005 after they sent my husband back. She has never seen her father.

He is in hiding somewhere now in a third country. It is in no way safe for him to return to Bangladesh. I am in touch with him as he phones me whenever he can, but I do not know where he is exactly or when we will be together again. My elder son is ten and he has lived through all this with us. He is scared for his father and misses him very much.

I can never go back to Bangladesh. My father is dead now, there is only my Mum. She can give me lots and lots of love, it's like she keeps me safe in her heart where nobody can kidnap me or criticise me, nobody can touch me. But she knows it is not possible for me to come back. Not only was I raped but my rape was reported in the newspapers, so everyone knows. Even she thought it might be better for me to commit suicide. Lots of relatives thought that if I did that everything would be finished, the disgrace would be gone. And I did think of it many times, but then I would always decide against it, because I do have rights, not just as a woman but as a human being. If my children get the right to stay here,

3. Dallas Court is the Home Office reporting centre for Greater Manchester where asylum seekers have to report regularly.

no one need know that their Mum was raped, but if they are in Bangladesh no one will let them forget it. In my country I also got violence from my in-laws. My mother-in-law stopped speaking to me, my in-laws rejected me and they wanted my husband to divorce me. If I go back they will never accept me back.

Perhaps if I get my status here we can put that behind us. Maybe I will always feel it inside me, but no one will bother about it. Yet if I get justice one day, what kind of justice will I get? The Home Office may give me status but will the people who kidnapped me get punishment? Will I get back the life that I lost? I will never get my life back again, the life I had before 2000. I lost something that I can never get back, even if my kidnappers are punished. They slashed my arms and they burned me with cigarettes but my hands are OK now, just there are some little scars. But inside me there is a horrible scar which cannot be rubbed out.

Another reason I am vulnerable in Bangladesh is that I have been involved in an organisation that is concerned with women's rights. In 1998 I wrote two books of poems that dealt with things like how women are treated, especially poor women, how they experience violence in their homes. The titles were 'You are a Secret in my Heart' and 'Not Hate but Regret'. I had criticized extremists and because of this I was accused of offending religion. But what is the use of claiming that you are a good Muslim and praying five times a day if then you go home and beat your wife? I don't know if all the people who criticised me actually read what I wrote. But I got a reaction in the newspaper – "Who is this woman writing like this? She is not a good woman." I got the same reaction from some members of my family; they said I should not write this stuff. But I am a writer, I create what I write from the feelings in my heart. I told them this is my matter and I write what is in my heart. But all this means that I have a profile in Bangladesh, it would be impossible now for me to live anonymously there.

Men have cheated women of their rights – but I am not one of those who believe that all men are bad. Men need women and women need men so why should I hate men? I would really like to write more about women's rights, but my situation is such that I cannot at the moment. I write from my heart and brain but my brain is burning. I have a thousand billion sentences in my heart and brain, so many ideas, but I left everything. If I write them all down it would be a library. If I get a good environment and a good chance I will write it all down, I will do this.

MARY

'The ADF is a rebel group that arose predominantly from the grievances of young disaffected Muslims and Baganda nationalists, which has operated in Western Uganda from bases in the Congo since 1996. The current government came to power with a clear commitment to higher human rights standards. Unfortunately it has been unable to maintain these… As the threats away from combat zones have grown since 1998, a new illegal system of detention by military agencies has been established, based predominantly on so-called 'safe houses'. This provides an environment in which other unlawful acts are carried out including… sexual abuse and rape.'

Report submitted by country specialist for Mary's case

I was born in Kampala in Uganda. We were three kids – one boy and two girls. I went to a nice school. I completed O-level. My Dad was a businessman. He was doing spare parts. When I completed O level I went to help my Dad. I trained in business with him. Then I got a boyfriend who became my husband. We got married in the traditional way. We started our own business. My husband was also a businessman, we moved in that kind of circle. So we decided to do another business, a pharmacy, as well as the spare parts business. We did this with the help of some pharmacists and doctors that we knew – there was a guy from Kenya who was supplying us drugs from Wellcome. We did it for quite a long time. We had good earnings. We had two kids. When my sister and her husband died of AIDS I brought her kids to my house. So I was responsible for four kids. They were in good schools, boarding schools. Our business was a family business; my husband had his people working with him. They would go and look for markets because in my country it is not like here where there is an ASDA in every place. We were in the capital and we had everything. It's the capital that supplies to villages. We were supplying medicines to other parts.

Now my husband had a brother we used to work with. That brother of my husband, he was a rebel. A rebel is someone who gets a gun and fights the government. He was dealing with rebels who were fighting the government, he was actually one of them, it was ADF (Allied Democratic Front). He was fighting on their side. But I did not know that at the time. Me, I just knew that he worked with my husband.

I didn't know about this because they didn't talk about it. My brother-in-law was, how shall I say, like a spy. A spy can be there and even his mother doesn't know he is a spy. I only knew that he went looking for markets and went for business. I just thought that he went up country but I was thinking it was for business. He used to go to the area in western Uganda near the Congo, where the rebel group was based. How could I know he was supplying rebels? My husband, I found out later that he knew, he had the knowledge of it. Maybe he was involved. You know, we Africans - for us the man is a man. If he decides to tell you something he can, but if not you don't ask him any questions. If he tells you that tomorrow I'll be going to somebody's place to do this – that's all! He may say I will ring you or tell you but if he has decided not to tell you then he will not. And when we are getting married they tell us you have to listen to your husband. That is the first thing you mother will tell you.

One day in 2003 a neighbour of this brother-in-law came and told us that "You know they have taken him away." Army men came at night and took him. We were wondering: why did they take him? But soon after that army men came and invaded the pharmacy. It was like… how can I say? Like a swarm of bees. We saw army men coming in our pharmacy. They started shouting, beating the workers, asking where the guns are, they started searching, taking things. Then they were beating me, pushing me. Then they took me away in their car to their 'safe house', asking me all the time where are the rebels, where are the guns. Me, I could say that I didn't know – because I did not know. But in my country if somebody is a rebel they take the family to be involved as well, they take the family to be rebels. So they took me. I was in a tiny room, with a cement floor and no windows, no toilet. I could hear other people crying and screaming and being beaten. I was raped there at least once a day, by different men. I was kicked, beaten, and they burned me with cigarettes. I was there for three weeks. I was bleeding a lot so maybe they thought I would die. They blindfolded me and took me and threw me somewhere by the roadside and they told me if you tell anybody what happened you are in for it. You will be killed. They do it in my country. Then they went away.

I was in great pain, shouting, crying, asking for help. A lady came by and took me to the hospital. I asked her to go to find a certain doctor whom we know, he had a clinic close to the pharmacy. When you get him tell him that Mary is in the hospital. For us, if you are in a serious condition, if you need medication, you need to have someone you know to help you. I thought he would make sure I had good treatment. So he came and he talked to other doctors he knew. They treated me and I had to have an operation. I stayed in the hospital for seven days When I was discharged I went back home. My husband had been advised not to open the pharmacy, but after a month, my husband said he was going to open the pharmacy, it would be OK. And it was OK for about two to three months.

Then it was the 13th November of the same year my husband took medicine to Rwenzori pharmacy. Now my real job at the pharmacy was to take money to the bank, see how much money we had got. Next day I went to deposit the money in the bank, but while I was there a neighbour who lived near the pharmacy called me and told me don't go back to the pharmacy, those people are back, all the workers are taken and the pharmacy is closed. I was thinking that maybe it would be like last time, so I decided to go to the family's spare parts shop. But even there I saw that they were beating workers. The army people were shouting, kicking, pushing, beating people so I did not stop, because I was in a taxi. So I went home, but before reaching home I met a neighbour. You know in Africa you may know everybody within in ten miles, it is not like here, everyone knows everyone. They told me, they are there, so don't try to go there. I tried to call my husband, his phone was off. So I decided to go to the doctor's home, the one who had helped me in the hospital.

That was when I realised that my brother-in-law is a rebel. Because I was asking the doctor what is going on, I don't know. All that time I had thought that maybe we were attacked because of jealousy of the neighbours or business colleagues. Anyway that is when that doctor told me that that boy is involved with rebel groups. I said what about my husband? He said you need to get out now, let me help to take you to that business colleague who supplies medicine from Kenya so that you can hide for a while. Once everything dies down you will be back. It was a day's journey to go across to Kenya. He left me at the border, where this colleague was waiting for us. We crossed into Kenya on foot.

Then the colleague took me to his place where I had to stay indoors - because why? Because those government people in Kenya, they get Ugandans and send them back. The Kenyan police support the Ugandan government. So I was in hiding in the house for a month, trying to find out where is my husband, what is happening. One day he told me, "I can't even keep you here any more because things are bad, your medicine, the boxes supplied by your pharmacy, were found in a rebel camp. So things are not OK. Supposing you are ill and I have to take you to the hospital, they will ask who are you. But I will see what I can do." The next morning he brought a man, telling me this man is going to take you where you will be more safe than in this place because you know what the Kenyan government and the Ugandan government are doing. He introduced me to this man, he said his name was Tunde and he said you are going to be Mrs Tunde, you will pass as his wife. They took my photos and in the evening the guy came with a passport for me. He showed me the passport saying, you are now Mrs Tunde. He said, "Don't ask where you are going, just follow that guy and he will take you to the place where I think you will be OK."

So he took me to the airport and before long I found myself in England. When we got off from the airplane they put me in a car or a taxi – me thinking that we are going to his home! They drove for four to five hours, and then they dropped me in Manchester to a place which now I know is Refugee Action. They said you go there and press the bell, we will go and look for a place to park the car. I pressed the bell and they opened the door. I was taken in and they asked me who are you, why are you running away? I told them all about the situation, I said someone has dropped me and told me you go there and they will help me. I don't even know if that man lived in this country. I have never seen him again. They told me at Refugee Action now you have to claim asylum, so I did that and they gave me a house to stay.

At this time I was bleeding a lot from the operation wound, especially when I was in my periods. The discharge was smelling. So they took me to the GP who gave me some medicine to take. But one day it was too much. I woke up bleeding so much, the sheets were wet. That is when they arranged for me to go to St Mary's. When I went there they said we can't wait, we don't know why all this is coming out of your stomach, but it is urgent and so you are going to be operated. So they operated me and after the operation the consultant told me they had taken out a lot of tissue, a tumour.

My asylum application was refused in June 2004, and one of the things the Home Office said was that there was not enough evidence that I had been mistreated or raped. So after the refusal I went to the Medical Foundation for the Care of Victims of Torture and their doctor examined me. They gave a positive report, it confirmed my account. After the refusal came, the solicitor arranged for an 'expert report' from somebody who was an expert on my country. The medical report and the country expert report were both consistent with what I was saying. There was no doubt. But when we appealed one of the things they said in the refusal was that I was lying because I must have known these people are rebels. But what did they want me to say? So they want me to lie?

.

The appeal failed though we sent all this evidence and now I have nothing. It's the end of the line. I have a campaign and my campaigners are trying to help me. Whoever looked at the case said it was a good case. Why did the judge refuse? He said he can't agree with the medical report but I keep wondering about this. I sometimes sit and cry. Now I can talk to people about it, but then I couldn't talk. In those days in 2005 you could talk to me and I couldn't speak because in my head there would be nothing there.

After my refusal I had nowhere to go. I would go to my friends but they were all scared because they were also asylum seekers. Sometimes I would sleep in doorways in Manchester. Sometimes I would walk up and down, and then go in a call box as if I am calling someone. Sometimes I read novels and books. Now I go to WAST and meet people. Once I went to the Red Cross and there I met a woman from Rwanda who became my friend. She is still fighting her case so she said I could stay with her. Then I contacted Emma Ginn at the National Coalition of Anti-Deportation Campaigns, she was shocked, she said she couldn't understand why they did not grant me permission to stay. That judge was funny; when he was refusing me his first sentence was that he had seen me and my husband give evidence but my husband is not even in this country. Since November 2003 I have never seen my husband or my children and I don't know what happened to them. I was told it was a 'slip of the tongue' but how could a judge make such a mistake? The judge admitted the medical report but said it did not change his mind that I did know about the rebels and my account was not credible.

The judge said she is a wife so she can go back and live with her husband. But in my country if they are looking for your husband they will also look for you. If I had not got out as I did I might have died and no one would have taken responsibility for my death. I can't go back to Uganda and I can't go back to Kenya either because they take Ugandans and they deport them, or they just disappear, they are killed. In Britain they know about Amin who used to kill people on the streets. It is not like that. This president is more intelligent, he knows how to kill. They come, they beat you or they look for you. Then you disappear and that is the end of you, they will bury you in the forest so no-one knows. And in my country whatever a policeman says is true, you can't contest it. If you do, the next day you are taken. So I can never go back to Uganda.

SIKHONZILE NDLOVU

Independence with majority rule in Zimbabwe (formerly Rhodesia) was achieved largely through the efforts of two main parties – Robert Mugabe's ZANU (which had its political base among the Shona people) and ZAPU led by Joshua Nkomo (with its base among the minority Ndebele people). For some years these groups fought Ian Smith's white minority government as guerrillas from bases in Zambia and Mozambique. Independence was won in 1980. Robert Mugabe became prime minister and later sacked Joshua Nkomo from his cabinet. The Movement for Democratic Change (MDC) was formed in 1999, born of profound dissatisfaction with Mugabe's repression and mismanagement of the country.

My name is Sikhonzile and I am coming from Zimbabwe. I am from Tsholotsho, a rural area, in Matabeleland. Now the problem we have in Matabeleland is that before independence the Ndebele people who live there supported Nkomo's party, ZAPU. Now Robert Mugabe's ZANU are in power, they don't like the people who are coming from our area. Mugabe will die in that mind set. Mugabe's government won't authorise anything for the Ndebele because they don't want any development on our side. Where I am coming from, the rural areas are still poor, it is no better than in Ian Smith's time, nobody develops it.

My parents were involved in ZAPU, they were politically active. My father was with Joshua Nkomo, imprisoned and then in exile in Zambia – it's a long story and I can't go into it now. They had done a little bit of farming. In the rural area you have to plough, you eat what you grow. If it is more you can sell your maize or sorghum or peanuts to the Grain Marketing Board in Bulowayo. We were doing that from time to time. My mother was raising pigs, and those pigs were helping us to get money to pay for us to go to school. But I could not finish school for money reasons. As my parents did not have any employment sometimes it was hard for them to pay our school fees. So I did not finish my O-levels. I ended up getting married, a traditional African marriage. That is, my man talked to my parents when he had seen me, then they agreed, they approved. My husband and I had three children.

But it was as difficult for us as it had been for my parents. I am an Ndebele and it's difficult for Ndebele to get work in Zimbabwe. You will go from Monday to Friday to get work but the Shona people will not employ you. They will look at your ears - the Ndebele have a special way of piercing their ears. We Ndebele didn't get so much education so we are the ones who go have to go to South Africa to get work. Our children in Matabeleland, they can't pass the public exams, they will get marked down. It's mainly Shona who do the marking and they can tell by the surnames that this is a Matabeleland person. The discrimination is not public and open but we all know it is there. People like me are seen as the enemy of ZANU wherever I go, because I come from the district where the opposition party is strongest, where it started.

That's why I went to Johannesburg in South Africa to try to find some work there to help my family. I started as a domestic worker. In South Africa many people have cleaners and nannies. Some are trained, some are not trained. You have to clean the house, cook and look after the children. They only pay a little bit of money. I did that as an illegal immigrant for quite a long time. I had to do it as an illegal because if I was to go through the whole process and apply for a visa I would never succeed. People of our tribe believe that originally we were South Africans, if you go back in history. The Ndebele people are really culturally similar to Zulu. When Zulu people talk there is nothing they say that I can't understand. In some ways I understand the situation in South Africa better than in Zimbabwe.

I worked as a domestic worker in South Africa for many years then I trained as a security officer. You start as Grade E and I trained up to Grade B. I was a security supervisor in big stores, so I know how to operate security cameras. The system of security is different from here, it's according to the rules of the country, and human rights are not the same. There we did body searching, which they don't do here. You search the body of the person with a special sensor.

I was working in South Africa for more than seven years, I would send money and I went back home sometimes with clothes for my children, I was struggling to take them because those Shona people in customs and immigration, they will search you like you are a criminal even though you bought all those things legally and you have your passport with you and all the receipts.

Most of the Zimbabweans in South Africa were illegal immigrants without visas. In South Africa we were not happy at all, we had to struggle to make sure we looked and sounded like South Africans – if they find out that you are a Zimbabwean and you are working they arrest you and put you in a big detention centre for foreigners, not only Zimbabweans but people from a lot of different countries. People are racist in South Africa - I am not talking just about the whites, the whites pretend to like the foreigners because they want the foreigners to work for them for low wages.

Crossing the border into South Africa from Zimbabwe is dangerous in itself for the illegal migrant. When Zimbabweans go to South Africa they don't go by cars or bus, they go by foot. Sometimes they use a truck but then sometimes the driver will drop them near a border post. They may get killed and there is no way to trace them then, people at home will be thinking you are in South Africa and anyone you know in South Africa will think you are still in Zimbabwe. But you are dead, disappeared; they throw them in the Limpopo River, the biggest river in South Africa that is like a border between South Africa and Zimbabwe. There are crocodiles and leopards, all kinds of dangerous animals so no-one will go looking for you. Sometimes we use another route by Botswana.

I started to join the Movement for Democratic Change while I was in South Africa because it was actually formed while I was out there. MDC emerged from Zimbabwe Congress of Trade Unions. MDC was committed to ending discrimination against regions or nations within Zimbabwe, that's what they promised the people. So I joined the group in South Africa and started going to meetings. I was selected as a female security officer. I was taking minutes for meetings for Austin Moyo; he was secretary for MDC in South Africa. The MDC has branches in many places, like in Manchester there is a branch.

MDC is not an illegal party in Zimbabwe, but the South African government is supporting ZANU so the MDC in South Africa is suspect and if they found we were meeting we might get arrested and they would hand us over to Zimbabwe. What we were facing was very hard but we were struggling to change things in our country. To tell you the truth we are not happy to have to go to find work all over the world when we have got our home, our own country. We would just like a normal life there.

One day I came out after a meeting. I was with my brothers Simon and John – they were also working in South Africa. We had a lot of leaflets to distribute in different places so that they would know about our party. We gave a passer-by a leaflet and then suddenly some men came and grabbed us, and after that day I never saw my brothers again. As for me, I was grabbed by two men, they took me to the park and they raped me and dumped me. I came to when a lady, a stranger, came past the park where they had dumped me.

That lady helped me to get back to my flat, but when I reached my flat I found that everything is upside down. All the papers were torn, and the cassettes we had been using in our fundraising drive were destroyed and all my money was taken. When someone does that to you, you get confused, you think what's going on, what have I done? Then I realised that the men who attacked us were the CIO - an undercover intelligence organisation, a ZANU organisation. When they were attacking us they were talking in a broken South African language, I could recognise a Shona accent. I went to the police station to report what had happened to me, but they said they can't help me because I am a Zimbabwean. They said it sounded like a political thing, they couldn't do anything about it, and I should go and report it in my country. But of course you can't report to the government what the agents of the government have done to you – no-one would listen to you. So I asked the police to at least give me an affidavit so that I could get treated in hospital, because to get free treatment in these circumstances you have to have an affidavit. They said no, we can't help. I ended up going to my cousin's sister to ask for money to go to a private doctor because I was badly injured. He treated me but he refused to give me a report of the treatment because he said I did not come with an affidavit.

When I was better I went back to work. But what shocked me, I started getting anonymous calls at work, people warning me not to carry on working with the MDC. They said they would kill me, they made all sorts of threats. It disturbed me so much I ended up not wanting to take a call of any kind. If someone at work said 'Sikhonzile, there a call for you' I did not want to take it because I would be afraid it was one of those anonymous calls. Also I did not want my work mates to be aware what is going on. I did sometimes grab the phone and when I heard those voices I would be in tears and I couldn't concentrate at work. And then when I went home after work there would be threat calls again. I tried to move around in South Africa but found that wherever I moved it got worse. They were watching me, they had got my picture, and all my documents because of course they had been to my flat. What really shocked me was when I saw my photo on the wall of a post office. It was like a kind of missing person notice, we are looking for this lady, you know what I mean. It had been put up by ZANU people. I felt really scared.

After I had left Johannesburg for Mpumalanga township I went back to Johannesburg to look for my brothers, to find out where had they put them, but I didn't find them. I even went to the morgues – maybe they are dead? I went to where they lived but nobody knew where they are. I tried to call back home and I asked my father to look all over the prisons in Zimbabwe in case they had been deported back, but nobody could tell us anything. I realised I myself am in great danger now.

I told people in the MDC meeting what I had been through and they said "You have to be strong because you have volunteered that you are going to change the situation in Zimbabwe. These are the kind of things you are going to go through, don't be scared of anything". But I thought I can't stand for that, so then I decided to get out. I asked my cousin to help me and friends and well-wishers contributed and in that way we got money together. I didn't care whether I went to Britain or somewhere else, I just wanted to escape and preserve my life.

My cousin got me a ticket for London and when I reached London I told them straight that I am seeking asylum. That was in 2002. It was very busy that day, so many Zimbabweans arriving. They could not attend to us all on the same day so we had to sleep in Heathrow for three nights on the benches. They made us wait. Any flights that were coming from Africa at that time were having five or ten Zimbabweans asylum seekers on board because the ZANU people were making it so difficult for people there, beating people up and victimizing them. Eventually they did attend to us and screen us. I did explain my situation at the port of entry.

I stayed only the three nights in London then I was relocated to a hotel in Kent. There we got some briefing, what goes on if you are seeking asylum, what stage we were at, which stage we were going to pass. I was given the number of a solicitor in Leicester. I went to Refugee Action there, but then they relocated me to Radcliffe in Manchester in 2003. I had a number of different solicitors while I was moving about, and I don't think my case was handled well. It all went wrong, and I was refused. They did not believe that I was an MDC member and they did not believe that I had been attacked. I challenged the refusal on my own without a solicitor but they said I didn't present enough about my political reasons. I don't know why, because whatever they asked me I did reply. So everything went wrong.

Now I am struggling to put in a fresh claim. This time the solicitor wants to stress my activities here, not just back home. I even asked my father to send a statement about how is their situation back home, and he did that, explaining everything, that at any time the security people of ZANU can come to the house, break the doors down and enter. They have been threatened many times. My fresh claim will be on the grounds of my political involvement here. I am still involved with MDC, we are still functioning well with monthly meetings. They let us use a room in a pub on the last Saturday of every month. We gather together and share all the things we plan. I get a lot of personal and emotional support from the MDC members in UK. At present I don't have any great hopes for change because we are by ourselves. Nobody wants to help the Zimbabweans. Both the Conservative and the Labour Party here know very well what is going on in Zimbabwe but they won't help us to remove Mugabe. There are many, many ways in which that man could be removed. But the government here, all they do is deport people back to Zimbabwe on the grounds that they are safe there while they know very well what is going on there. No wonder we don't succeed but we still keep trying to change things in Zimbabwe.

Since I left South Africa in 2002 I have never seen my husband and kids. My husband and kids keep moving from place to place because they think if the authorities know where they are living they are going to face problems. I am in touch with them. They can go to the public phone and call me, that's how they let me know where they are except that one is now in South Africa and I can't get hold of him, my first born, he is 22. The other sons are in Zimbabwe they are 20 and 16. I always feel that I am a bad mother to my children because I ran away from them. I left them for many years. I didn't manage to bring them up myself. I wanted to give my children good principles. Every mother has her own values to pass on to her children, but me, unfortunately I couldn't do that. I don't know how I am going to bear that all my life. How can I present myself to my children as a good mother? I do love them as much as I could. If they could see me giving speeches, telling people what we are facing and why I came here maybe they might feel proud of me, but then I am still the one who put them in a bad situation in the first place through my political activities.

I have just joined computer classes but I don't know how much I am going to learn because sometimes the information just enters there in my head and comes straight out, I can't concentrate. I forget things all the time – and I used to have a very good memory. If you are a mother... sometimes I am at the computer and it as if it clicks onto something in my head, something about my children and why am I here, and then I ask myself what is the use of doing all these courses. Then everything I have learnt goes out of my head. If only after I finish my appointment with you I could go home and chat with my children, or if I could go over their college work with them...but now I don't even know my children's character, what each of them is like now, and they don't know mine any more. I can't tell you! My sisters will tell them your Mum is a person who's like this or like that, I don't even know if they believe what they are told – it must be like they are talking about some stranger, the lady from down the road maybe. I don't know how I am going to make my relationship with my children. This makes me very unhappy and I wonder if I will end up mentally disturbed.

I remember that my Mum told me that whenever you get things happening in your country you mustn't go and seek help in any other country. She remembers that we had such a difficult life when my father was away in Zambia fighting with ZAPU. It took ages and ages for me to tell her that I am an asylum seeker in Britain, that I am struggling to be a refugee - because she did warn me. She told me before that you must never, never seek help from neighbouring countries, you will suffer. It is very painful to be a failed asylum seeker like me, very very painful. Now at my stage all the support I have got is from the Red Cross who give me food and a bus pass. I have no entitlement to NASS accommodation, I am hiding myself under my friend's roof. Sometimes I am in Openshaw, sometimes in Bolton, any friend of mine who will offer me a shelter. I just live from day to day. But how long can a person survive in this situation?

4

NOWHERE IS HOME

Politics in the modern world is often dominated by ethnic competition. Even conflicts which are not explicitly about ethnicity may have an ethnic dimension, as we saw in the case of Sikhonzile's story. It is common for one ethnic group to try to consolidate its dominance in a particular area. The means used may range from discrimination to intimidation, to murder or even massacre. This has led to widespread population movement in areas like the Balkans, and to waves of refugees. In many cases the refugees have no obvious alternative place that they can claim as their 'homeland' and even if they have, there is no guarantee that they will be able to settle there. When Eritreans started to be expelled from Ethiopia, Asli's family was scattered and still has only been partially reunited.

Another category of 'homeless' refugees are groups that as a result of conflict or past political re-alignments have effectively no citizenship in any country of the world and are forced to lead a marginalised existence with little prospect of betterment. Such is the case of the 'Biharis' in Bangladesh, as Nilofer's story shows.

ASLI

Eritrea won independence from Ethiopia in 1993 (it had previously been a part of Ethiopia). Since then there has been hostility between the two countries, and a border dispute issue erupted into war in 1998. People of Eritrean descent resident in Ethiopia, who had formerly enjoyed the same rights as other Ethiopian citizens, were now made to carry identity documents defining them as resident aliens. As a result of harassment and discrimination many fled and tried to cross the borders into Eritrea or other neighbouring countries. Many were arrested and deported by the Ethiopian authorities.

My family are originally from what is now Eritrea but I myself was born in Ethiopia. Ethiopia and Eritrea used to be one country before. People moved from one city to another freely, it was all called Ethiopia, so my parents came to work in Addis Ababa, the capital. My Dad used to have his own garage and we were quite well off. We were quite a big family, five children, and four step-brothers and sisters from another relationship my Dad had had before. I went to school and I did a French course. Something a bit different from the other students. My Dad always thought it was good to do something a bit different from everyone else because there are not enough jobs in Ethiopia, a big percentage of unemployment. If you can offer something different from the rest, if you have been to university, you could have better chances of getting a job. My parents were quite ambitious for us. I was in college when we left. I did not get as far as university. My mother was like many African women; her husband was in work so she did not need to work and she had plenty to do looking after all of us kids. She never went to school.

In 1998 there was a war between Eritrea and Ethiopia. So all Eritreans living in Ethiopia now had to leave Ethiopia and go back to their other home. But this was difficult because everyone had made their own homes in Ethiopia, had their children there and had no connections in Eritrea. Many of the businesses in Addis Ababa were owned by Eritreans. In 2000 my Dad was arrested and taken to the police station and I don't know what happened after that. They were grabbing Eritrean people from home or work. My Mum went to the police station to find out what was happening and they also put her in prison for a day, then sent her back saying be prepared to go back to Eritrea. Whole Eritrean families were being expelled. So my Mum came back but we don't know what happened to my Dad. Since then I have never seen him. I only learnt that he died after we came to Britain. My Mum was frightened because they were also grabbing people. They couldn't easily tell whether a young person like myself, dressed in T-shirt and trousers, was Eritrean but older people like my Mum, they could tell from the style of hair, the way they dress. But more was happening in the capital than in the villages so my mother sent us to stay with our grandmother (her mother) in the country.

I went to my grandmother's place along with my sister Abeba and my brother Gabriel. My mother sent us because we were the eldest, the younger children stayed with her. We didn't know what had happened to all the people taken by the authorities. We stayed a while there but my grandmother was so afraid that we also can be taken. She said it was better to move to another country. So she took five of us with her – myself, my sister Abeba, also my step sisters Marie, Asmeret and Sintaye. We travelled to Djibouti. This time we stayed in a small village just over the border from Ethiopia. We moved there because there were other Ethiopian immigrants there.

At that time we thought my mother might join us there. We were not the only ones fleeing. People were being split up, some to Sudan, Kenya, Djibouti. People just went where they could so that the Ethiopian authorities would not catch them. We only went to Djibouti because it was near to where we had been staying. We did not even get to the capital. We just crossed the border and stayed in a small village there. If you were lucky enough to be able to cross the border you just had to stay where you were until you could find a way to get to the city, or until you could get money to pay for transport. We had to live like that, on the streets. We just lived by begging to get anything to eat. I could not go to college, and my sisters could not go to school. I have very bad memories of that time. When you are young you want to enjoy yourself, but that was not possible for us at all. We just had to survive somehow. We stayed there three years in all.

Soon after we arrived my grandmother got sick. She had TB. I feel like I am responsible for her getting sick, she died because she was so sick. She was not in good health to start with and all this hardship was too much, she had just had to leave with us kids. Now I had to do something to support my sisters; when people see a mother with young kids they will take pity on her and give her something to eat, but not a young person like us, so I and my sisters had to go and find some work. I had to fill our stomachs somehow so that we could eat. During that time my two step-sisters Asmeret and Sintaye took off because they could not live like that. I don't know where they went. To be honest, I think they went to the city. They were younger than me, just kids. I didn't want them to go but I couldn't control it. I was only 20 years old at that time. The two sisters who were left came here with me.

I worked for two years for someone who had his own wife and kids, just doing cleaning and housework, a housemaid. They paid me hardly anything. My sister got work as a housemaid in return for something to eat for her and my other sister. In the village where we stayed I went to church there and got to know people. My family are Christians, but it was not easy to go to church and follow your faith in Djibouti because it is a predominantly Muslim society. Sometimes my sister and I had to find excuses to go and meet the Catholic sister at the church. We knew she might be able to find some contact to find our family. So she introduced us to the priest, who contacted the mission in Addis Ababa. One of the priests contacted another priest in Addis Ababa and they traced my father's business partner. He was not an Eritrean but he helped us a lot because he felt he owed it to us. He paid for false passports for us. He was the one person who knew what had happened to my Mum and he told the priest she was in Britain with two of my sisters, Sissay and Dahab, though he did not know exactly where she was. He helped us to get a ticket to go to join her.

It took a long time to trace my mother but the priest helped us. I took a plane with an agent, along with my sisters Abeba and Marie. We did not know how the agent was going to get us to Britain. But we were arrested in Belgium because our false passports were spotted. That was a horrible situation, an awful experience; we thought are we ever going to get to the UK and see our Mum? The system there is a bit different from here where you get NASS accommodation, and they took us to a kind of detention centre. There were other young people there and we were there for two months. The woman from the Belgian authorities traced my mother through the Red Cross and they found her. The social worker there was really good. We were able to speak to our mother on the phone and when I heard her voice I could not believe it was her. I don't know what she said, she was just crying. The social worker who was with us could not make out what was going on and asked us what was she saying? She could only hear her crying on the phone. I still couldn't believe I was going to see her again until we met her here.

The Home Office allowed us to join our mother and sisters in the UK, and provided us with tickets and travel documents. At first they had told our mother, through the solicitor, that they were ready to allow only my step-sister Marie to join her, because she was under eighteen at the time. Then my Mum's solicitor pointed out that the other two were her blood-related daughters and pressed that we should be allowed to come also. As I understand it, the Belgian Home Office had got in touch with the British Home Office. They had not expected the British Home Office to accept us since the Belgians never accepted refugees from UK, there was no treaty or agreement. So I don't really know what happened, but the Home Office in London agreed to accept us on the travel documents provided by the Belgians. The plan was that we would be met by a Home Office official at Heathrow and that our claim to asylum would be joint with that of our mother.

The Home Office had contacted my Mum and said do you want to come down from Manchester and meet the girls or do you want to receive them in Manchester? She came down, she said she couldn't wait, so she came to meet us. The plane arrived late at night and an official from the Home Office was supposed to wait for us, but no-one was there. So we showed our travel documents and the immigration officers asked us to wait. They took us to an office and started asking questions about how and why we had arrived. We tried to explain but we could not make them understand. One of the immigration officers told us that they were considering us as new-coming refugees claiming asylum. So they made us sign papers as though we were claiming asylum independently, instead of linking us with our Mum's case. She had already been given asylum and our names were on her files.

So we signed the claim for asylum and that was a big mistake, though we did not know it at that time. We did not know anything about the system. My Mum and my sister Sissay were waiting outside, but of course they could not do anything. Sissay tried to call the Home Office and tell them that we were already at Heathrow but by that time the immigration officials had done the screening for us and opened a new file for us. They treated us as though we were claiming asylum on our own, as three separate young adults, not part of a family. My Mum had already put in a claim in 2000 but nothing was done on her file until 2003. In October 2003 a family amnesty had arrived and she was granted asylum under that. But we arrived in December 2003, just two months too late to be included in that.

I didn't live with Mum at first. Because we were over 18 they gave us separate accommodation. Anyway she only had two rooms, she was living there with my younger sisters. In 2005 they stopped support for Abeba so now we only had £71 a week for three persons. I was still supporting her. Now they have withdrawn my support too. We are destitute now and living with my Mum and she supports us. If the Home Office refuses us, she will not be able to accommodate us legally.

I have completed an Access course and my next step would be to go to University. That's what I would like to do. I am really interested in business studies. I get that from my Dad. I actually got a university place but I could not take it up as I had no status. I carried on studying IT and accounting but now I have stopped. There seemed no point in signing up for courses when I did not even know whether I would be allowed to continue next September. To sign up for a college course you have to show that you have support from NASS, and there is no point in studying if I can't continue further to higher education. So I am stuck!

"My asylum application was refused because I wouldn't identif the woman who was my girlfriend"

VICTORIA

Ever since we left home we have been like blind people being
led along, never knowing where each step will lead."

HUMMERA

"I have a thousand billion sentences in my heart and brain, s
many ideas... If I get a good environment and a good
chance, I will write it all down." **NAIM**

Sometimes I would sleep in doorways in Manchester. Sometimes would walk up and down, and then go in a call box as if I am alling someone."

MARY

"I don't even know my children's character, what each of them is like now, and they don't know mine any more."

SIKHONZIL

"We have been told that the Home Office might be using our case as a 'test case' and that is why they have been especially harsh with us·'"

NILOFER

"My life here is just as difficult as it was back home."

EMIOL

'I have this dream that my daughter could finish off school and maybe be able to support herself and support me as well."

IVY

As I stood at the plane door I felt fear that my husband's family may have discovered our plan to flee, as well as grief at all that e were leaving behind."

FARHAT

I also do some voluntary work at Rainbow Haven project and the Black Health Agency and of course I work as a volunteer with WAST. Also my sisters and I have a campaign started and I spend some time on that. I would like to enjoy myself as a young person but I can only do this if I do not have the worry that I will be deported. Young people here are lucky, they do not know anything about the things we have had to go through.

I try to be busy to try to forget all my troubles. Keeping busy helps me to forget, but tears are never far from my eyes. We came here because of persecution, because we had to look for somewhere that could be home for us. I have nowhere to go. I have been refused to become an Ethiopian and asked to leave. Eritrea is a place I have never been to. Maybe I know the language but I have never been there and I do not know any people there or have any contacts. It would be as if you who grew up in Britain were suddenly asked to leave for America or Nigeria or India where you don't know anyone. I definitely feel that Manchester can be my home now because all the family that I have are here. Home is where you feel you're safe with your family. As long as I do not have Leave to Remain I cannot have peace of mind.

NILOFER

In 1947 the former British dominion of India achieved independence as two separate countries, India and Pakistan. Pakistan consisted of the uneasy union of two geographically separate territories – West Pakistan and East Pakistan, both dominated by Muslim populations (East Pakistan consisted of part of the former province of Bengal). Many Muslims from Bihar, an eastern province of India, migrated to East Pakistan at that time. In 1971 East Pakistan became an independent country, Bangladesh, after much bitter conflict. Many of the Bihari community in East Pakistan had been against this separation and some had actively aided the Pakistani army when it attempted to suppress the liberation movement. After the birth of Bangladesh, members of the Bihari community (also known as 'Stranded Pakistanis' since they still regarded themselves as citizens of Pakistan and have not been allowed Bangladeshi citizenship) were herded into 66 camps where they live in conditions of great deprivation. Some Biharis now wish to have full Bangladeshi citizenship, others still seek to emigrate to Pakistan, which has been reluctant to accept more than a few. Numbering about 300,000, they remain a stateless and oppressed minority whose fate has yet to be resolved.

My family originally came from India, from Assam in the north-east of that country. My father was a master tailor. My family had gone to Bangladesh in 1947 (at that time it was East Pakistan). At the moment some of my family are in Bangladesh, some are in India, and some in Pakistan. Those people who had come from India were called Biharis in Bangladesh because Bihar was the area in India where most of them had come from originally. I have five children. The youngest was born here in the UK.

After the 1971 war, when East Pakistan became Bangladesh, my family wanted to stay in Bangladesh. After all I was born there. But we had become a minority people; the Bangladeshi people saw us as traitors because many Biharis had sided with Pakistan in 1971. They looked down on us and they treated us very badly.

My father and father-in-law had favoured Pakistan, also my husband. Many Biharis had helped the Pakistani military in 1971. A few Biharis were allowed to leave and go to Pakistan, but then they stopped accepting them. The rest of us were left behind. We were herded into camps but we were despised by Bangladeshis. They said "If you don't like it here just go to Pakistan."

So we lived in Dhaka in a big refugee camp. Our life was not good there, we had so many problems. There was a school in the camp but it was not adequate for the children and they did not learn much. All the age groups were mixed up in the same classroom. They only learnt very basic stuff, no English or even proper Bengali.

There was not much work for Biharis either. My husband used to work part-time but he did not earn much. The camp was isolated from the rest of the city and we had to use agents to find work. If the broker got 100 taka then the worker would only see 30 taka – so we only got a fraction of what we really earned. But my husband did a lot of community service for the Biharis in the camp.

We women mostly stayed inside the camp. Some could make a little money sewing clothes or selling cooked food which would be delivered to factories. I sometimes used to earn a little money this way. It was dangerous for us to go outside the camp, especially for girls, so we could not go and deliver the food ourselves. So people used to make money out of us. And when people saw the food coming out of the camps they thought we must be earning thousands of taka – they would extort money from us and beat us if we did not give it. No use telling them that it was the middleman who was making all the money. But at least we were able to survive.

One day my husband was outside the camp and some men from a well-known gang pulled him off his bike and demanded money. They said, "Give us the money or you are not going anywhere." They said "If you go to the police we will get you and bury you alive." What could he do? We Biharis could not say anything, and we knew we would not get any protection from the police anyway. If we went to them they would not write anything down, only demand bribes from us. The persecution of this gang was one of the things that decided us to try to leave Bangladesh.

We came here because an agent got travel documents for us. This was five years ago. The deal was that we would use the false documents and then hand them back to someone in London and receive some money in return. When we came we had no idea where we were going to stay or what we were going to do. When we arrived at the airport in London we were just wandering about, we had no idea where to go. We did not understand the currency and we were speaking Bengali. So someone directed us to Whitechapel because that is where Bengalis in London live. But when we got there we still did not know what to do. We had kept back a little of the food they had given us on the plane, but by now we had eaten that. In the end a Bengali man came up and started talking to us. He asked us where do you want to go. He took us to a shop and got us some food. My husband explained everything to him. In the end he let us come to his house and he showed us how to get a solicitor and ask for asylum. People who have been living here a long time know the system, but at that time we knew nothing.

Our friend could not take us in as his house was already overcrowded so he sent us to stay with some relatives of his in Birmingham. We stayed there for a few months but it was not good. My children's education was interrupted and my son could not sit his A-levels.. While we were in Birmingham we went to the Asian Resource Centre and they helped us a lot. We met John O from the National Coalition of Anti-Deportation Campaigns there and he started a campaign for us. Lots of people signed petitions that we should be allowed to stay.

When we had made our asylum claim it was refused at first but eventually we were given Exceptional Leave to Remain. But then the Home Office appealed against this decision and they won. (We have been told by our lawyers that the Home Office might be using our case as a 'test case' and that is why they have been especially harsh with us). By this time we had been dispersed to Manchester and my children were at school there.

They tried to deport us in September 2004. My husband refused to board the plane without proper documents and confirmation that the Bangladesh government would accept an EU travel document. He said he would go back to Bangladesh if they would accept him but he was not going back without his family. The chief stewardess looked at the papers and then a Sikh gentleman who was a passenger translated for us and explained what my husband was trying to say. Even the pilot came along and asked what was going on. He looked at our papers and said, "We can't take this man, these papers will not be accepted in Dhaka," and he took away the boarding card. Perhaps they had had difficulties with deportees being accepted before. The plane was ready to leave and we had to get our bags and get off and then the immigration people started to be very rough with us and they even slapped my husband. They took us off and locked us in a room. Then a lady came and she was a little more polite. My youngest son was only a baby and he was crying and crying. They had not let us have water or anything. After a while two men came in, one English and one Asian, and they let us out but not my husband. So we went out and phoned our friend in London and he took us to the lawyer. As a result of that my husband got bail but he was still locked up for three weeks.

We have been living in Manchester for some time now and we have built a strong family life here. My husband just wants to get Leave to Remain and be able to get a job and be independent. If only he were allowed to work – it is not good for a man to sit at home all day. My sons have tried hard to integrate, they have been involved in voluntary community work and one of them gives advice at a community advice centre, he has received an award for his activities. The children just want to study and get on with their lives.

Wherever we go, we Biharis are suspected. We have no status in Bangladesh but those who have gone to India are not secure either. Some have been put in jail because they accuse them of being spies. We applied to both Bangladesh and the Pakistani government to allow us in. The Bangladesh High Commission said they will not accept us back. The Pakistan High Commission says that we are 'Stranded Pakistani Citizens' but that repatriation of Stranded Pakistani Citizens has not yet been settled. So they would not issue a passport either. So it seems that we do not really belong anywhere.

5

THE RIGHT TO HEALTH AND SUPPORT

Article 25 of the United Nations Universal Declaration of Human Rights states that everyone 'has the right to a standard of living adequate for health and well being of himself (sic) and his family including food, clothing and medical care and necessary social services, and the right to security in the event of unemployment, sickness, disability, widowhood, old age or other lack of livelihood in circumstances beyond his control.' Clearly few governments guarantee these rights in any complete sense. In many parts of the world, there is little provision for the disabled, and disability may be a source of stigma and discrimination, as Emiola's story shows to be the case in Nigeria. Ivy is fleeing from Malawi to avoid what is in effect a forced marriage but her circumstances are complicated by the fact that she is HIV positive and if she is deported back to Malawi she will be unable to access the drugs that are ensuring her survival. She will also suffer the stigma associated with HIV status.

EMIOLA

'There are no laws that prohibit discrimination against persons with physical and mental disabilities… there are no laws requiring accessibility for persons with disabilities. Children and women with disabilities face social stigma, exploitation and discrimination and were often regarded as a source of shame by their own families. Children with disabilities who could not contribute to family income were seen as a liability and in some cases were severely neglected. Significant numbers of indigent persons with disabilities begged on the streets.'
Nigeria: Country Reports on Human Rights Practices for 2006, US Department of State. Released March 2007.

I was born twenty-three years ago in Nigeria, in Lagos. It's a big city; it used to be the capital of Nigeria. I've got one brother, older than me. My Mum still lives in Lagos. I would say that my family were poor; my Mummy does not have a specific job, she just sells sweets on the street, things like that. My Daddy was a carpenter but, you know, when somebody is illiterate they have to work very hard, it is hard for them to progress.

I had polio when I was just one year old which left me paralysed from the waist down. I had to use callipers and crutches to get about. Before that I had been fine; my Mum told me that I had walked at the age of seven months. Yet as a result of this my Mum rejected me, she said that she couldn't take care of me, it would be too much stress and she didn't have money. She absolutely rejected me. They say that my Mummy even tried to poison me. But my Daddy took care of me, he accepted me in spite of my disability. That is what separated my Daddy and my Mummy. They split up while I was still a baby and my Daddy brought me up. I can't remember them splitting up, all I can remember is that I was with my Daddy when I went to primary school and secondary school, right until the time he died. My brother normally stayed with my Mum though at times he came to my Daddy's place.

I know it is difficult to take care of a disabled child in Nigeria, so I believe that my Daddy did a great job. I really appreciate him for all the care he gave me. He accepted me the way I was. That was really a happy time. I went to primary school, then secondary school up to the age of fourteen years. When I was in grade three of secondary school I stopped because that was when my Dad died. There was nowhere for me to go, so I had to move back to my Mummy's. She was not happy about this but she had no option but to accept me. She would give me instructions, "Don't do this, don't do that, stay indoors." If her friends were coming to visit her she would even lock me inside because she didn't want people to know that she had a disabled daughter, something like that. That is a very common attitude in Nigeria. Parents feel ashamed if their child has a disability. And if you are disabled it is hard to get married. You hardly ever see someone married to a disabled person. The family will not allow them. When I was in school I wondered if I would get married, but I thought that if I did it would be to another disabled person because that person would give me joy more than an abled person. They would be there for me, they would not look down on me. There would be equality. That is still at the back of my mind even now.

When I moved in with my Mum she told me I would have to stop going to school because she didn't have money to spend on me. So from that time I just stayed at home. If there was food in the house I would eat. At times there was not and I had to get some from other people, manage like that. In Nigeria the houses are often facing each other, close together, so people know if you need help. Another thing was that I got help from people at the church where I started going. And that was what brought more hatred from my mother, the fact that that my family were Muslims and I was going to change to Christian. She did not want to allow that so in that area we fought a lot. She was not happy with me and when her friends came she used to hide me inside. In the end she threw me out and I had to leave.

Now the primary school that I went to was for physically handicapped children, a special school. The lessons there helped me a lot, to look at more things in life. That's why I was always confident. They would tell us that there are disabled people who go to university, who are working, they encouraged us to think "Me too, I can do that, I can be independent." That was just in my mind that I could take care of myself. But it was not that easy. When I left my Mummy's house, I would stay wherever I could. Sometimes I would sleep in the church if there was a night vigil. Or if there were no service and the church was not open at night I would go on the streets and just help myself as best I could. In that church they did help, but if your own family does not accept you, if your Mummy is still alive but she does not accept you, other people will not offer to give you a home. So the only thing I was getting from the Church was that I could get somewhere to sleep.

Because I could not finish my education I could not get a job, I just had to beg. It was through begging on the street that I survived. People don't want to look after disabled people but they don't mind giving. There is a saying in Nigeria, people will give you fish to eat but they won't teach you how to fish. So people will give you little bits of money or food, but they won't help you become independent. I had lots of friends on the street there. I remember that in my refusal letter from the Home Office they said why can't I go to any organisation in Nigeria, but I knew from the experience of my friends on the streets that they don't give you any real help. There are too many disabled people for them to take care of. And the second thing is that many of them are not really taking care of them, they are just doing it to get money, using them to raise funds. So people beg on the streets to survive for their life.

Most of the time I used to sleep in a part-completed building. It had no bathroom or toilet, and I even had to pay to sleep there. I had to go behind a bush to go to the toilet, and I was only able to wash myself three times a week. Where I was sleeping it was open to anyone to come in and once I got raped there by someone who came there at night. I did not know the person who did that to me, but I discovered that I was pregnant. I endured an abortion which I had to pay for myself as there was no one else to help me.

There was a man who used to see me regularly on the streets. At times he would give me food, at times money. He just picked me and took an interest in me. He would sit down with me and we would be talking, talking, talking. And he was a Christian as well. He used to say that one day he is going to help me. One day he came to where I was staying and he took my picture and took my name and date of birth. He got some papers for me and a passport for himself, and he told me that we were going to travel on such-and-such a date. He told me to get ready. So I travelled with him and we came together to this country in 2005.

We arrived in London; we stayed in London for some days. And then he told me that we are not going to stay in London, that we are going to another city, we would be moving to Manchester on 9th August. We came to Manchester together on 9th August. When we got to the bus station he told me to wait, he would be coming back with his friend. But they did not return. I was waiting there for ages, from 12 in the morning to 11 at night. He had abandoned me. In fact I never saw that guy again. I was just crying because I didn't know what to say, or what to do, I didn't know where to go. Luckily for me I saw two policemen passing and I asked them for help. They took me to the police Domestic Violence Unit and they got me accommodation for two days. On the third day they filled out a form for me and said I should go to Refugee Action.

I sought asylum in August 2005, but on 5th September my application was refused. I find it difficult to understand why it was refused as even the judge himself said that he found my account credible. He said in his determination, "If Emiola returned to Nigeria her prospects will be awful." He said that it was very likely that I would end up living in the same circumstances that I was living in when I left. The judge accepted that the Nigerian police force suffers badly from corruption, is poorly paid and is not a police force that could be looked to for protection against rape or redress from rape. I appealed on grounds of human rights and that one was refused also.

Then my solicitor was able to submit new evidence and I made a fresh claim but that one was refused on October 26th 2006. My solicitor said they might take the case to judicial review, but the barrister's opinion was that there are no grounds to seeking judicial review; there was no error of law in my case. But they said that I might make a further fresh claim if I can get more information together, more evidence from Nigeria that there is no assistance for me, lack of social services, discrimination against disabled women.

When I first arrived in this country it seemed to me like I am in paradise. I could not believe it, I was so happy. I thought at last I am going to do something with my life. That was my hope. And it is still my hope, but it is so hard. The first flat I was given here was at the top of fourteen stairs. So for ten good months in this country I could hardly move outside. If I complained they said because I was an asylum seeker they couldn't change it, that I had no choice. They couldn't do this and they couldn't do that. Then I did not think I was in paradise, at that time I thought I was in hell! If it was not for the members of the church I belong to I don't know what would have happened. The members of that church would come to my flat to see me. Then they (NASS) moved me at last and now I have a ground floor flat and I can get in and out fine. When I was in Nigeria I did not have a wheelchair, only some crutches and callipers. Now I have a wheelchair and can get about better, though sometimes there are problems with the buses. I remember two or three weeks ago the driver had to carry me onto the bus because it was the last bus in the area and it was not a 'low liner', so I could not get my wheelchair onto the bus.

Now I don't think this country is either heaven or hell. It is just like most places - somewhere in-between. But if I can stay here I do have a chance to do something with my life which I could not do in Nigeria. I have been studying at college for my European Computer Driving Licence, and I think I have the ability to do it. The problem is that while my case is not settled I find it difficult to concentrate. When we had a test everyone in the class passed, it was only me that failed. I was not happy about it, I was so discouraged. I don't believe that I am incapable of doing it but I am always worrying about my case and whether the Home Office will send me back so it is difficult for me to study.

I don't really have any contact with anyone in Nigeria any more. I have no family there who can help me, no one to go back to. But I have now got quite a lot of friends here, especially from my Church. But the people who give me the greatest support are WAST. They really, really try to help me. Before I came to WAST, when I was in the other flat and I got the first refusal letter - I just cried. There was no-one to give me encouragement. The people at the church I was going to at that time didn't believe in politics or campaigning or anything like that, so they could not help me in that respect. WAST encouraged me to set up a campaign and I got people involved through WAST. Also people got involved through seeing my story on the National Coalition of Anti-Deportation Campaigns website. Now, any time I need advice I think, "Let me go to WAST, you will get advice, you will get encouragement there, and a sense of relief."

IVY

One in every seven Malawians is living with HIV or AIDS. The Malawian government launched a National AIDS policy in 2004 and is committed to providing free anti-retroviral drugs to everyone who needs them, but a major problem in combating AIDS in Malawi is the shortage of trained medical personnel who can administer the drugs, especially in the public sector. One of the reasons for this is that so many Malawian doctors and nurses have emigrated to take up better-paid jobs abroad, notably in the UK. The human resources crisis means that many HIV/AIDS sufferers in Malawi cannot get the treatment they require to stay alive and healthy. Anti-retrovirals need to be accompanied by a good diet, yet malnutrition is common in Malawi and this is another factor which hinders attempts to stem the AIDS epidemic.

I was born in 1965 in Blantyre, southern Malawi, the first of ten children. My father was a hospital doctor and my mother a housewife, looking after the children. After school, I copied my auntie and went to college to study dressmaking. I bought a tailor's shop in the town and later my next sister worked there with me. In 1985, I married a boy from my choir, who I had convinced to attend my church despite him being a Muslim. He was only the seventh-born so he had some freedom to choose these things, although to start with his parents were not very supportive of our marriage because they didn't want him to marry a Christian. You could say he really was a Christian – God's word touched him. He was so caring and even took my family as his own. He became like the second-born in my family. My husband was a businessman as well, with a trans-African haulage business.

My daughter, Sulita, was born in 1986. I decided to have just one child because my husband and I were the main breadwinners for our family once my father had retired. He farmed some land but had to pay school fees for all those children, so I helped with most things including teaching the young ones and making clothes for everyone. I also took two of my mother's children to live with me, so it was like I had three children. It was a busy but good life. But then, in July 2002, my husband died in a car accident.

In Muslim culture, a ceremony is held forty days after the death and on that day, his family said, "Look here, you have to marry your husband's brother so you can stay in our family". I didn't like the man, who was much older and already married with four children. He had been my husband's business partner and, because they knew how much my husband had supported them financially, my parents agreed, even though it was against our religion. They were only interested in what they could get from the marriage - they wouldn't listen to me at all.

So I ran to some friends, away from Blantyre, although I knew they could easily find out where I was. My friend didn't want to shelter me because she was afraid of my relatives. Meanwhile, the brother was angry and ordered that my daughter be sent to him. My father thought it was OK, because it would make me come back. I had a cousin in the UK, and I told her my whole story. I called her, and she said I could come for a break, to get away from this situation. So I contacted my sister at the shop and advised her to sell some of my sewing machines. I told her I was leaving and warned her not to tell anyone. She put the money in my account and I bought a ticket. I came here in November 2002 on a visitor visa. I was coming for a holiday on a visitor's visa, but I also secretly thought maybe I could just stay here. I thought it was easy just to come and live without any problems, I didn't know how my cousin was living in this country. I thought, "I am not coming back home." I could forget all my past and carry on with my life.

When I arrived, I was refused entry. They asked how long I was visiting for and although in my mind I was thinking that I'm not going back, of course I did not say that. So I said, "For three months" – it just came out of my mouth. They did not believe it was a genuine visit and called up my cousin. "She says she's coming to visit you for three months, but she's going back today because she can't." She asked if she could come and see me, and came from Luton and asked me what was going on. Then I was put in detention at Heathrow.

There were a few others in there, and this lady from South Africa kept talking about asylum, asylum, asylum. I was so depressed, I cried the whole day. I didn't know what was happening, because they wanted to send me home, but I couldn't go home. In the evening I fell ill and instead of boarding a plane I ended up in hospital. I just collapsed and the next morning I was in a different place. They said they had examined me and seen a shadow on my chest which showed I might have TB and they needed to keep me in for checks.

A friendly nurse asked how I had got there, and when I explained she said, "The story you've told me, if you had known you could have said 'I'm seeking asylum', not 'I've come to visit for 3 months.'" We haven't got any asylum seeker issues back home so I didn't know I could do that. She told me about asylum. Then two weeks after my admission I was asked if they could test my blood, and I tested HIV positive as well. It hadn't been the normal TB.

I was discharged in December and went to my cousin's place in Luton. I told her what had happened and that I needed a safe place. In Africa you don't just tell anybody about HIV because they'll say 'She's got AIDS and she's going to die any time', but she was so nice. Also, the nurse had found out about where I was going and which law centre I could attend and so I already had a solicitor, who wrote to the Home Office, who called me for interview. I told them my story and they said "We understand but we don't believe you. There is medication in Malawi, so you should go home." They refused my case. I went for the second hearing because my solicitor appealed, and they refused again.

By then my daughter was here. When my brother-in-law realised I had left the country he had begun mistreating the poor child, and she had run away to my sister. But she already had three children. We were still in touch and she said she couldn't look after my daughter, so I asked her to sell some more stuff and send Sulita to me. She came in 2003, July. I was so happy because I'd thought I was going to die before seeing her again. The doctors had told me I'd be well as long as I took their advice and medication, but I hadn't believed it, because most people back in Africa, they die of this HIV. They said this medication is for life, once you have started you mustn't stop, but you are going to be OK, but I thought they were just saying it. My solicitor told me to invite my daughter. She said I couldn't go home now that I had started the medication. She said "Your daughter hasn't got anyone and you need a carer." I was the person who received her at the airport. I was very happy to see her. She was sixteen then and therefore could still be considered as my dependent.

After I was refused I had to find a private solicitor to write my appeal to the tribunal, and at the same time I received a letter from NASS that they were giving me accommodation in Manchester. We lived there from November till June, but when our case was again refused we had to leave our NASS accommodation. The George House Trust, an organisation for people living with HIV, found me somewhere to live in Crumpsall through social services, because they support people who've got health problems and they don't care about your refugee status. But social services don't want to take responsibility for my daughter because she is now over eighteen. It's so depressing at the moment. I need my daughter to live with me as a carer, and she's my only family. She is my mother, my sister, she is everything, and she is now being refused to live with me. It's like nobody cares about her. I can't send my daughter to live in the street! My cousin in Luton has two children and no husband, so she can't look after her.

Social services give me £78 every two weeks, and it's a one-room studio flat. Neither of us is allowed to work, and I have to use it for bus money for her to go to Stockport College, four buses every day. When we moved to Crumpsall she couldn't change school immediately. Because I volunteer at George House Trust and am a service user, they sometimes give me a little something to keep me going. And they also registered me with the Red Cross where I go once a week to collect food.

My daughter is studying health and social care. It's a bit difficult for her because she doesn't want to tell people who she is. There are issues about asylum seekers; it seems as if they are not considered human. She has friends, but even those who she visits or who visit my flat, they don't know why we are living in this country. You can't just tell anybody, you don't know who you are telling. She is the only one who knows about the HIV. I took a long time to tell her, I waited until she was eighteen. She knew I was not well and took tablets all the time, and probably saw some of my literature, but she couldn't ask me. African children are always polite – if you don't tell them something, they don't ask. But since I told her she has been so supportive. She says she is just happy to see me alive because she knows there are so many people who have died back home.

At the moment I'm still at the same place. I know where I'm coming from, but where I'm going I'm not really sure. I have a solicitor who has put in another fresh application and I'm waiting for that, and, being at the end of the line, I started my campaign, which is backed by the George House Trust. I have this dream that my daughter could finish off school and maybe be able to support herself and support me as well. But at the moment asylum seeker children cannot go to university, and she doesn't have her own campaign or court case yet.

Sulita understands that with this HIV thing, you need love and to be well-cared for. We are advised at the hospital that it is dangerous to worry or work too hard, or your CD4 count will go up and down. So she tells me that where I am, she will always be, and that if she marries she will stay nearby and take care of me with her husband. But I feel terrible for what all my own problems have meant for my daughter. If she sees me unhappy, she reassures me, but I think, "What am I doing to her?" It troubles me most of the time.

I try to make myself busy because if I'm just at home, I don't know what to do or what to think about. I am one of the founders of WAST. We wanted to have something of our own and to choose a name. I'm quite happy to be involved on the committee and as the chairperson. At WAST we are all asylum seekers working for the same thing.

We go to church in Oldham. They are very supportive, but sometimes you feel useless when people just feel sorry for you and give you stuff. I don't like this kind of life. I've been independent since I left my parents' home. I was always giving out, now I'm just receiving. When the pastor calls you and gives you £20 from the offertory, I don't feel good about it. If I get my human rights, I will contribute something. I'm a dressmaker so I could make stuff for people. I do miss my tailoring a lot. There is a machine at George House Trust and whenever I see any nice pieces I try to make something. I adjust things which are too big or long and make my cushions and curtains. I miss it as my profession, miss having an income, but I'm still doing it. I'd also quite like to work for a charity, because I have been helped myself by different organisations and know I could give a lot to them.

You know, when I was back home, just to hear of England, I thought it was heaven. Back home, people from England are treated like angels, with so much respect. I thought I would be treated the same here, which is not true. If I'd known, I wouldn't have chosen to come here. I would have gone to America or somewhere else. I've really had an experience here. If I ever had a chance to go somewhere else, I don't think I'll say anything good about the UK. Sometimes I think if I'd gone somewhere else, maybe things would have been different.

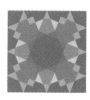

6. BEING AN ASYLUM SEEKER: A CRIME

By Emiola Fadeyi

Asylum Seeker is not the end of the road.
We are human being
We are women of great expectation.
We are women of vision.

Even though back home
I am the most wanted
Sometimes I feel like I'm grounded from being
Safe and peace-minded.

Asylum Seeker is not the end of the road.
Our journey to this country is not an excursion.
Our loneliness is unbearable,
We are lonesome,
We are lonesome.

To any traveller, any place we come to can be home
Even for a day or two.
Any language we learnt can be our own
For as long as we care to use it

Asylum Seeker is not the end of the road.
When I stretched out my hand
No one was there to grab it,
Because I am an asylum seeker.
When I looked back I felt bad because
People called me *Asylum Seeker.*

Then I wept bitterly because no one was there
To call me by my name.
They used reference number.
They called me *E1034873.*

Asylum Seeker is not the end of the road.
I wish I could feel 100 % happy
But I can't, some things never leave your mind.
Freedom is not just about not being killed,
Freedom is having choice in your life.

But thanks to Asylum Seeker Project, like WAST,
Because of their support
They made me forget
About how people can be so cruel and ignorant!

We are strong women
Doing the best we can do.
One day the rain will end
And a light of sunshine
Will shine on top of our head.

GRANTED! GRANTED! GRANTED!

7

WHY WOMEN SEEK ASYLUM – AND WHAT THE ASYLUM SYSTEM DOES TO WOMEN

By Ursula Sharma

Good news for women?

In 1999 the House of Lords heard the appeals of two Pakistani women asylum seekers. Mrs Shah had been turned out of the marital home in Pakistan by a violent husband who threatened to denounce her for the alleged crime of sexual immorality. If convicted she could be sentenced to 100 lashes or death by stoning. Mrs Islam had worked as a teacher in Pakistan and after she had intervened in a fight between students of rival political groups, members of one group told her husband that she was an adulteress. She was assaulted repeatedly by her husband and sought refuge with her brother, who received anonymous threats as long as she stayed with him. Both these women had fled to the UK in fear for their lives, but both had had their applications for asylum refused by the Home Office.

The landmark ruling of the House of Lords was that women may be deemed to constitute a 'social group' under the terms of the UN Refugee Convention of 1951 and that therefore asylum could be granted to a woman if she was fleeing from forms of persecution specific to women in a particular country and from which the state offers no protection.

With respect to another set of House of Lords appeals[4], Baroness Hale had this to say in 2006:

The world has woken up to the fact that women as a sex may be persecuted in ways which are different from the ways in which men are persecuted and that they may be persecuted because of the inferior status accorded to their gender in their home society.

United Kingdom House of Lords Decisions 2005-6 UKHL 46

Previous significant decisions were made in 2000 when the Home Office issued gender guidelines aimed at informing those who adjudicate appeals, and in 2005 when the Home Office issued policy instructions intended to inform all stages of the asylum process. These guidelines recognise the many forms of persecution and oppression which are specific to women as well as the problems which women may face in seeking asylum.

All this should have been good news for women asylum seekers. Yet many women who have clearly suffered from gender persecution are still refused asylum. Often they are simply disbelieved, or are told that they should resettle in a different area of their own country. Many women who have suffered rape, torture and domestic violence, who have been persecuted for challenging regimes or practices oppressive to women, who have been threatened with genital mutilation or punished for their sexuality are deemed to be 'failed' asylum seekers and forced into a destitution that is often little (if at all) better than the situations from which they have fled. The stories of the women of WAST illustrate this insensitivity and injustice only too well.

4. Those of K, an Iranian woman harassed and raped by Revolutionary Guards, and Miss Fonah, a Sierra Leonian fleeing from the threat of female genital mutilation.

Rape as punishment, rape as control

A striking feature of the stories in this book is that practically every one of these women had at some time been raped (even gang raped) or otherwise sexually abused. A woman may be raped as a punishment for her political involvement (as in the case of Sikhonzile who opposed the Mugabe regime in Zimbabwe) or for that of her husband or relative (as in the cases of Naima from Bangladesh who bravely refused to reveal her husband's whereabouts to his political opponents, or Mary whose brother-in-law was suspected of aiding rebels in Uganda). She may be raped by a husband as a form of revenge or control, like Victoria who was forcibly married, in an attempt to control her lesbian tendencies.

Other women experience sexual abuse when they are in a vulnerable position due to lack of family support, separation from family, or destitution for whatever cause. Asli was abused by her employer when she had no source of income other than to work as a maidservant. Emiola was raped while living on the streets where her disability forced her to make a living by begging.

Where the experience of rape is an important aspect of a women's application of asylum, the burden of proving it lies with her. Concrete evidence of rape is generally difficult to produce, especially if it is required long after the event. (Sikhonzile could not get the affidavit she needed from the South African police which would oblige a doctor to report on her condition). Frequently the authorities are in collusion with the perpetrators or prefer to turn a blind eye to the offence.

Lack of protection by the authorities

Women's accounts of rape and domestic violence have only come to be taken seriously by police and courts in this country relatively recently. Here and elsewhere, offences against women have often been trivialised and women have been disbelieved. When she tried to leave her violent husband, Victoria was told by the police that her problems were a 'family matter' and of no concern to them.

Some of the women who arrive in the UK as asylum seekers come from areas where the state has 'failed' or where civil war makes protection and security hard to come by for any citizen. In some places the state itself defines women as a separate category of citizen and expects them to abide by different and usually more oppressive rules than men. Hummera fears to go back to Pakistan since if the validity of her marriage were challenged she could be charged with the crime of adultery.

Lack of family protection

In most parts of the world the family constitutes a safety net for both men and women in the absence of an established welfare state. This becomes even more important in periods of political breakdown, yet that is precisely when families are liable to be dispersed. Asli's father disappeared, presumed dead, during the period when the Ethiopian state was persecuting Eritreans living in Ethiopia. When it became necessary to flee Addis Ababa, she and her siblings were dispersed. She was eventually reunited with her mother and sisters in Manchester but her application to stay in UK has been refused. Victoria lost her father when he fled from the rebels in Liberia; her mother became dependent on her aunt and thus could not give Victoria the suport she needed.

Violation of gender norms

Women are also liable to lose the protection of the family when they are regarded as having transgressed local gender rules. Naima's rape was thought to have brought disgrace upon her in-laws' family and they have rejected her. Hummera knows that she cannot go back to her family in Pakistan, having made a love marriage against the wishes of her parents, who have effectively disowned her. Even leaving an abusive husband may be seen as a violation of social norms, as Farhat Khan, the founder of WAST, has found; her family was unable to give her any support and she had no option but to leave for a safer life outside Pakistan. Naima has also been castigated for writing poetry that was interpreted as anti-Islamic and fears that if she returns to Bangladesh this profile would make it impossible for her to settle, even supposing her other problems were solved. Victoria's uncle rejected her because of her lesbianism and was not prepared to help her escape from a violent forced marriage. Ivy's flight from Malawi was a response to pressure from both her own family and her in-laws to follow the custom in her husband's community and marry the brother of her dead husband.

Political activities

Women may be persecuted for their own political activities, as in the case of Sikhonzile who continued to organise for the Zimbabwean Movement for Democratic Change in spite of threats against her life. They may also be punished or persecuted for the political affiliations of their husbands or other male kin, or for acts of rebellion which their men folk are supposed to have perpetrated. Mary was raped because her brother-in-law was alleged to have assisted a rebel group in Uganda, despite being adamant that she knew nothing about this. Naima was raped because she would not tell her husband's political opponents where he was.

Return and relocation?

The Home Office may determine against an asylum seeker if they hold that it is possible for the applicant to settle in a different part of their own country where they will not be liable to persecution. But this is to overlook the reality of life for women in many parts of the world. Farhat Khan, who founded WAST, is an educated woman who worked in a well-paid job in Pakistan, albeit against her violent husband's wishes. He subjected her to many beatings and tried to force her to give up her work. Had she not left he would have succeeded in forcing her daughters to marry against their will. When Farhat's case was adjudicated it was acknowledged that she did indeed experience violence at the hands of her husband, but the Home Office ruled that she might safely return to Pakistan to live in a different area. Even for an articulate and educated woman in Pakistan, this is a totally unrealistic supposition. Firstly if (as in Farhat's case) the persecutor is a powerful and well-connected man, he or members of his family may be able to track down the victim of their persecution quite easily. Anonymity is not an option. Secondly, in a country like Bangladesh or Pakistan, a woman living on her own with no obvious local connections is liable to attract (at best) suspicious attention and (at worst) harassment. She does not conform to ideas about the proper moral location of women in families.

Down and out, courtesy of Her Majesty's Government

The media tend to represent asylum seekers as though they calculated to come to the UK because this country is 'soft' on asylum seekers and gives them better benefits than many other countries. Popular discourse about asylum is dominated by the bugbear of the 'bogus' asylum seeker who fabricates stories of oppression in order to enter this country and enjoy its economic benefits. According to this stereotype, asylum seekers live in comfort at the expense of the British taxpayer. And then there are the urban myths, such as asylum seekers being issued with mobile phones by the government. In fact, as their stories show, very few of the WAST women intended specifically to come to this country. In the cases of Emiola and Mary it was a matter of what an agent or friend could manage to arrange for them; they were not the ones who made the choices and in fact these 'friends' effectively abandoned them once they arrived here. Naima and her husband fled to Jamaica before they eventually sought asylum in Britain. Nilofer and her family would have liked citizenship in Bangladesh or Pakistan best of all but, denied that, would welcome the opportunity to settle and contribute to the community in Britain. Victoria only came here, as she thought, en route to the USA.

The stories recorded here show just how ludicrous the stereotypical views are. Though some (like Nilofer) have come from very poor backgrounds, others (like Naima and Farhat Khan) come from privilege. Is the level of support that asylum seekers receive really such as to provide an incentive to migration? Even those fortunate asylum seekers whose claims are accepted and who are eventually granted refugee status generally have a very hard time. They have to start their lives again from scratch and even once they are in a position to look for work they may find that their occupational qualifications are not accepted here, or that imperfect English is a real barrier to employment and integration.

The road to refugee status (for those who actually achieve it) is one of poverty and hardship, and destitution awaits the majority of those who are refused. A newly-arrived asylum seeker in this country depends for accommodation support and minimal financial support on a Home Office agency. Until April 2007 this was the National Asylum Support Service (NASS) and currently it is the new Borders and Immigration Agency (BIA). At the time of writing this support amounts to an allowance of £38 per week for an individual plus some kind of housing (frequently in a very run-down and even dangerous area). An asylum seeker has no choice as to where he or she is sent; some are 'dispersed' without warning to another city, or moved from place to place within the same city with little notice and no regard for any networks of support they have managed to establish. This is particularly disturbing for children like Victoria's son Scott, who continues to have speech problems which she attributes to this constant movement from pillar to post. Nilofer's sons have also been frustrated in their education by having to move around the country.

Once a claim for asylum has been refused (as the majority are) and any appeal rights exhausted, the claimant is normally no longer entitled to BIA support unless they have children under the age of 18 living with them. The claimant then becomes destitute, dependent entirely on the goodwill of any friends they may have (it is often other asylum seekers who allow the 'failed' asylum seeker to sleep on their sofa or spare bed), or on the handouts of the Red Cross or other voluntary organisations. The majority of asylum seekers will not be eligible to work legally in this country. Under an EC directive promulgated in 2003 an asylum seeker may apply for permission to work. However, this is subject to the proviso that s/he has already waited for more than 12 months for a decision from the Home Office, that the delay is not the asylum seeker's fault, and that the asylum seeker has an ongoing claim, at whatever stage. This of course does not help the 'failed' asylum seeker who has exhausted any right to appeal and who has not submitted a 'fresh claim', which is the situation of most of the women in this book at the time of writing. In short, those who are denied the right to work are those who are least likely to have other sources of support.

The scale of this destitution and its consequences cannot be underestimated. The total number of destitute asylum seekers in the UK is probably over 35,000 and according to Refugee Action at least 1000 refused asylum seekers are living in destitution in Greater Manchester:

They have no recourse to public funds, including job seekers allowance and housing benefit, and are not allowed to work. Increasingly other public services are being withdrawn, including healthcare and education… Many are supported to some extent by their own communities, who are some of the poorest communities in Greater Manchester. Over 300 food parcels are given out weekly by voluntary and faith groups in Greater Manchester and this does not meet the demand.

Refugee Action Manchester 'Briefing on the Destitution of Refused Asylum Seekers in Greater Manchester' 2006

Besides money, many social and civic benefits flow from having a job, above all the chance to manage one's life independently. Lacking that independence, no wonder Victoria complains of feeling like a 'slave'. It is largely through work that we extend our networks, make friends, and develop our sense of worth as citizens. Many asylum seekers, denied the chance to take paid work, do voluntary work in local organisations. Active participation in WAST has itself been a great source of satisfaction to some of the women whose stories feature in this book, both from the activities they undertake themselves and the support they receive from others. This kind of participation can give them self-respect and also provide an opportunity to maintain or develop skills. Those who have been able to enrol at local colleges may find satisfaction in further education, but anxiety and depression are not conducive to constructive study. Many, like Emiola and Sikhonzile, find it hard to achieve what they would like to.

The time it takes; the painful search for justice

No one should suffer destitution in an affluent country, least of all destitution imposed by law. But the poverty which asylum seekers experience is prolonged by the asylum process itself. Asylum legislation and the regulations which the Home Office follows in its decisions about specific cases or countries are constantly being revised so we this book does not try to summarise the current legal situation. Broadly speaking, the changes have been in the direction of greater restriction. There has been a stark contradiction between New Labour's populist desire to reduce the number of successful applications – and if possible to reduce the number of potential asylum seekers coming into the country in the first place – and any considerations of fairness, humanity and appropriate legal process.

Most of the women whose stories are recorded here had little advance knowledge of how the asylum system in this country works and consequently were ill prepared for the evidential requirements of the Home Office. (Victoria had no idea that her well-intentioned protection of her American friend's identity would count against her or that she might have to prove that she was a lesbian.) Even if they did know these requirements, the circumstances of their flight would generally have made collecting the right kind of evidence difficult if not impossible. They are caught in a process which is based on the notion that they are probably lying and that they must prove their 'credibility' according to rules which they have not had the opportunity to study in advance. Any small discrepancy or any lapse of memory in a story of flight under stress and conditions of persecution, any omission of a detail whose relevance they had not realised, can be seized upon to deny their credibility. The interview process itself is painful when the asylum applicant has to recall traumatic and violent events such as rape or torture. An article in the British Journal of Psychiatry, based on research with asylum seekers who had suffered sexual violence, notes that subjects frequently showed dissociative symptoms, flashbacks, avoidance of thoughts or feelings associated with the trauma and difficulty in disclosing personal information.[5]

Some refused asylum seekers are able to gather new evidence and are permitted to make a 'fresh claim', but this is not necessarily more likely to succeed than an initial claim. If we add on the time taken to process appeals, judicial reviews or fresh claims, the whole painful journey – from initial claim to final outcome is typically a matter of years. To illustrate this we have included Farhat Khan's 'time line' in this book. This particular story ends well, for the time being at least, since Farhat was recently granted refugee status and Leave to Remain for a further five years. But at the time of writing none of the other women in this book has reached that stage, nor is it certain that they ever will.

It has been acknowledged by the Government itself that the process has often been highly inefficient and slow-moving. Since March 2007 all new claims for asylum have been processed according to the 'New Asylum Model'. However, whilst this model cuts down the time taken over the initial decision there are serious concerns as to whether it leads to decision-making which is either more just or more sensitive to the real circumstances of asylum seekers.

Lives in limbo

It will come as no surprise that many of these women suffer from clinical depression and rely on antidepressants and sleeping pills. Their lives are in a kind of limbo and they have no means to move forward. In as much as an asylum seeker is still 'in' the system with a chance of her claim being accepted, the legal process demands that she go over her story many times,

5. '*Impact of sexual violence on disclosure during Home Office Interviews*', Bögner D, Herlihy, J and Brewin, CR. British Journal of Psychiatry 191 75-81. Summary at *www.medicalnewstoday.com/articles/75832. php*

rehearsing the violence and suffering that drove her to leave, commonly causing flashbacks and extreme stress. For those whose claims have been refused there is the fear of deportation and a return to whatever violence and persecution they have fled from. All asylum seekers are required to report to a special centre (usually every week) as though they were criminals, and some are even subject to 'tagging'.

For many, the indignity of being branded as liars (which is what it amounts to when the Home Office decides that an account of torture, rape or extreme deprivation is not 'credible') is a source of bitter grief and humiliation, as Naima's testimony shows. In addition to this, many have lost loved ones in the course of conflicts that caused them to leave their countries, or have lost touch with their own children so that they live with grief or guilt. Some, like Naima, are separated from husbands or partners, unsure whether or when they will see them again. Some have to deal with the trauma that their children have suffered whilst others, like Hummera, dread what may happen to the children if they are deported. Of all the women in this book, only Nilofer and Hummera live with their immediate families intact.

Perhaps one of the bitterest sources of suffering for these women is the stigma which attaches to the very term 'asylum seeker' in the popular mind, and the humiliation which this adds to their other problems. Farhat Khan describes how her children often asked her why she had asked for asylum when asylum seekers were regarded as so undesirable:

> Whilst attempting to explain why we had had to, I also try to deal with the loss of self-esteem and self worth that I am beginning to feel as the reality of being an asylum seeker sinks in.
>
> *Extract from essay written by Farhat while training as an advice worker*

Children and young people are especially vulnerable to the effects of this stigma, especially when it is added to the racial abuse they may receive in the playground or harassment on the streets.

A system which denies people dignity and gives them no choice but to live in grinding poverty surely adds cruelty to the injuries and sorrows they have already suffered. It is a form of inhumanity which we should not tolerate. The women of WAST hope that their stories will move you to do whatever is in your power to end it.

8

THE TIME IT TAKES:
FARHAT KHAN'S JOURNEY

The loss, the grief, the humiliation and the despair…
The resolution to fight back, the struggle, the support and the
regaining of hope…
The time and the effort it takes…

November 2000

Farhat Khan and her children arrive at Heathrow Airport in UK. They have fled Pakistan after more than ten years of domestic violence by Farhat's husband and his family and her two youngest daughters being forcibly engaged by their grandmother to cousins at five and seven years of age. Farhat became a victim of domestic violence mainly because of her husband's opposition to her work which does not conform to society's expectations of a woman's traditional role in the North West Frontier Province of Pakistan. Farhat has worked for twenty-one years in community development in Pakistan with the poorest of the poor, her work focussing mainly on women. In her last three years in Pakistan she worked for the Department for International Development (DFID) of the British government on an agenda of women's empowerment.

The family claims asylum at port; asylum claims by her two older children are to be considered separately from Farhat's claim because of their age. The family is mistreated at the airport with the immigration officer threatening to send them back to Pakistan on the next plane and making comments like, "No one flees with so many suitcases." Farhat Khan is accused of trying to tear their passports up even though she submits them to the immigration authorities. The family is forced to remain at the airport till 1.30 am despite the youngest child running a high fever and the family having been on the run for more than twenty-four hours. Farhat Khan and her eldest daughter are instructed to report to the immigration office at the airport at 8 am the next day for detailed asylum interviews. The interviews continue throughout the day despite the two being exhausted. They have not slept during the last forty-eight hours, and are traumatised by the ordeal of fleeing their home and country, and the treatment at the airport by the immigration authorities the evening before. Their solicitors lodge a complaint against this treatment with the Home Office. The family stays with friends in London while awaiting NASS support. Farhat Khan's three youngest children are six, seven and nine years at the time.

February 2001

The Khan family, comprising Farhat, her adult son and daughter who made separate asylum applications, and her three youngest children, are dispersed to Manchester by NASS. After spending the whole day on the road and then waiting at the bus stop in the freezing cold for four hours so NASS can locate appropriate accommodation for a family of this size, they arrive at a three-bedroom house at 11 pm. NASS has not made any arrangements for food and the support worker leaves with a warning that the area has a high crime rate and they should avoid going out in the dark. The family is so terrified that they insist on keeping their house boarded up for the next six months and pile up sofas and suitcases against the two exit doors every night.

May 2001

The immigration service complaints cell responds to allegations of mistreatment on arrival in the UK, by saying that the Immigration Officer in question had been interviewed and had "denied charges of abusive behaviour." The immigration officer admits that she had had difficulty in comprehending how Farhat Khan could have managed to bring such a large amount of luggage when she had claimed to have left home in such a hurry.

September 2001

Farhat Khan enrols for training in benefits advice and begins to work as a volunteer advice worker at the Cheetham Hill Advice Centre.

May 2002

The Home Office gives a negative decision on Farhat Khan's application for asylum. The decision, dated 29/03/01, is received in May 2002 after repeated requests and finally a threat of judicial review by her solicitors. The Home Office, in its decision, states that as Farhat's husband no longer resides in Pakistan, the Secretary of State "does not see any reason for her to fear repercussions from him should she return to Pakistan". The issue of the two younger girls being forced into marriage is not given any consideration. Farhat is shocked at the Home Office decision as, in spite of the way her family had been treated by immigration authorities on arrival, she had expected her application to be considered more sympathetically. The family's solicitors lodge an appeal against the decision.

July 2002

The Home Office Farhat Khan grants permission to work.

September 2002

Farhat Khan starts paid work at Manchester Refugee Support Network as a refugee projects support worker. She agrees to pay the Home Office £92.00 per week as this is the amount she earns above what she would receive from NASS. She is heartbroken when she receives news of her father's death in Pakistan.

December 2002

The appeal is heard at Manchester's immigration appellate authority. Farhat Khan and her supporters are shocked at the way she is treated by the adjudicator and the fact that a clerk is not present to record the court proceedings. They know that short of a miracle there is very little possibility of the adjudicator overturning the Home Office decision to refuse asylum.

February 2003

The appeal is refused by the immigration appellate authority. The adjudicator, in his determination, accepts that Farhat Khan had been subjected to substantial violence in the past but claims that the family would be safe if they relocated to another part of Pakistan. He also considers that her two daughters will not be forced into marriage as Farhat's husband or his family will not be able to trace her and the children if they relocate. The family's solicitors submit an application to the immigration appeal tribunal for a further right to appeal.

Farhat Khan starts working at the Cheetham Hill Advice Centre as a paid, multi-lingual advice worker.

April 2003

An application to the immigration appeal tribunal for a further right to appeal is refused; Farhat Khan is informed that she has no grounds for a judicial review.

May 2003

Farhat Khan and her children make a decision to fight for their right to stay in the UK. The 'Farhat Khan and Family Must Stay' campaign is launched with the help of friends and supporters and the National Coalition of Anti-Deportation Campaigns (NCADC). Throughout the summer Farhat and her children, friends and supporters campaign at different events in and around Manchester, collecting more than 10,000 signatures in support of the petition to the Home Office for their right to stay. Thousands of people write letters of support to the Home Office and to the local MP. This overwhelming public support helps to further reinforce Farhat Khan and her children's dogged determination to have the Home Office accept the credibility of their asylum claim. Campaign supporters include their local MP Graham Stringer, the leader of Manchester City Council and over fifty councillors, the Bishop of Manchester, Baroness Helena Kennedy and film director Ken Loach.

March 2004

Farhat Khan's permission to work is withdrawn by the Home Office. She continues to work at the Cheetham Hill Advice Centre as a volunteer; her family is forced again into being entirely dependent on NASS support. Clients, staff and the local councillor stage a demonstration outside the centre to protest the withdrawal of work permission; the event is covered by local media.

April 2004

The campaign presents petitions and letters of support to MP Graham Stringer at an event at Albert Square attended by scores of supporters, including the leader of Manchester City Council, Farhat's local councillors and local media.

June 2004

Graham Stringer presents a petition with 10,000 signatures to Des Browne, the then immigration minister, along with further representation by the family's solicitor. Browne refuses to use his discretion to grant Farhat Khan and her family leave to remain on compassionate grounds; his reason is that he considers that "Farhat is a strong woman who survived violence in Pakistan and has run such a big campaign in the UK, she can go back to Pakistan and easily start a new life anywhere in Pakistan." He grants one concession to the MP, saying that if new and substantial evidence is made available, a fresh asylum application may be put in.

August 2004

Fresh evidence in support of Farhat Khan's case is submitted to the Home Office by the family's solicitor. The fresh asylum application is based on the grounds that Farhat and her children will be at an even greater risk if returned to Pakistan as her husband and his family consider that Farhat has brought shame and dishonour to them by taking the children to Britain without their permission. The huge bundle that forms the fresh submission includes evidence of continuing harassment of Farhat by her husband in the UK, and his frequent visits to Pakistan.

December 2004

Farhat Khan and her three children are asked to attend a travel document interview at Dallas Court, the Home Office reporting centre. The interview is conducted by a senior official of the Consulate General of Pakistan in Manchester. Farhat objects to the presence of the Pakistani official as it breaches her right to confidentiality (as per the UN Convention on Refugees); she is warned by an immigration officer supervising the interview that she is liable to two years imprisonment if she refuses to comply. The Pakistan consular official asks for detailed information about her life in Pakistan, including names and addresses of relatives. When asked why this information is required, the Pakistan consular official states that she needs it to confirm that Farhat and her children are Pakistani citizens. The official has not been informed about the Home Office being in possession of the family's original Pakistan passports. She refuses to continue the interview when Farhat informs her that a fresh asylum application has been submitted on her behalf. By then the official has taken down many details about Farhat and her children, and her family in Pakistan. Her three youngest children have been fingerprinted and photographed. The family has been forced to sign applications for Pakistani travel documents. Farhat Khan's solicitor faxes a copy of the fresh submission; the immigration officer in charge of the interview apologises and explains that more than thirteen files exist in different Home Office offices and therefore 'mistakes can happen.' Farhat Khan is reassured to read that her files in Dallas Court have the words 'low security' written on them which she takes to mean that the Home Office does not consider that she or her children will abscond in the near future.

Farhat Khan receives an invitation to attend a Christmas reception at Buckingham Palace in recognition of her "significant recent contribution to national life." The invitation creates a big interest in the media, both national as well as local, as it highlights the contradiction between the treatment given to Farhat by different parts of the establishment - Buckingham Palace honouring her for the work she is doing while the Home Office takes steps to initiate the removal process by arranging for travel documents. The media coverage includes BBC Radio 4's Today programme, The Guardian and various national and local TV channels and newspapers. The news is also picked up by the Pakistan media who report the story more negatively.

Farhat Khan attends the palace reception along with her former boss from the British Council in Pakistan. Before being allowed to attend, a senior palace official advises Farhat that, "The media has probably misreported that you will ask the Queen for her help with the asylum application. It would not be appropriate to raise the issue with the Queen as she cannot interfere in political matters." Farhat Khan and her boss enjoy the reception, bemused at the bizarre situation of a failed asylum seeker rubbing shoulders with the high and the mighty. The queen says hello to Farhat Khan and asks her where she has come from. Farhat decides to be discreet and not have any further conversation, realising that the Queen has already done her bit for the campaign through the publicity generated as a result of the palace invitation. Farhat has no choice but to give a short briefing to Prince Edward on her grounds for asylum, as he questions her in detail about her background. Starting with the question "Where do you originally come from?" he continues to query her about how she has come to be in the UK. She nervously looks over her shoulder while answering him, not sure if the 'censorship' imposed on what to say to the queen applies to the prince also. Many of the other guests, including Bill Bryson and Ian Botham, recognise Farhat from the media coverage and offer their support.

January 2005

Farhat Khan is devastated to receive news of her mother's death in Pakistan. She finds it difficult to cope with the loss of both her parents, especially as she was not with them during their illness and at the time of their death.

April 2005

Farhat Khan leads a march from North Manchester to Albert Square. The march is part of the European Day of Action to demonstrate against the detention and deportation and of asylum seekers. The march is attended by hundreds of people.

May 2005

Farhat Khan wins the BBC GMR Volunteer Award 2005 in recognition of the impact that her learning as an adult has had on her own life and those of women from the local and the wider refugee and asylum-seeking community in Manchester.

June 2005

Farhat Khan's solicitor puts in a further representation to the Home Office regarding the wide media coverage the Buckingham Palace invitation has generated both in the UK and in Pakistan. He points out that this heightens the risk to Farhat on return, not only from Farhat's husband and his family but from those members of the public in Pakistan who may perceive Farhat's asylum claim as a challenge to existing societal norms and traditions.

Farhat Khan becomes one of the founder members of Women Asylum Seekers Together (WAST), a self-directed and self-help support group of asylum-seeking women from different nationalities who are facing deportation. The idea to set up such a group comes from Farhat's own experience as a failed asylum seeker and from meeting other asylum-seeking women through her work. WAST is officially launched and Julie Hesmondhalgh from Coronation Street becomes WAST's first patron.

October 2005

Community Service Volunteers (CSV) present Farhat Khan with Year of the Volunteer 2005 regional award in the category 'Inspiration'. The purpose of the awards is to "showcase the most inspirational volunteering stories in England in order to recognise the amazing work of volunteers and inspire more people to volunteer." She is one of 2005 recipients.

November 2005

Farhat and her children take a leading part in a demonstration against the detention and deportation of asylum-seeking children. Her forteen year old daughter gives a heartrending speech about why the family had to flee from Pakistan and how asylum is affecting her and her other siblings.

February 2006

Farhat Khan's solicitor makes a further representation to the Home Office regarding the current legal and political position of women in Pakistani culture. He highlights the laws surrounding honour killings and the Pakistan government's failure to repeal the infamous Hudood Ordinance 1979, a set of Shariah laws that have been widely used to discriminate against women.

Farhat's solicitor petitions the Home Office to grant her permission to work, on the basis that more than a year has passed since a further representation was submitted to them and no decision has been made.

Graham Stringer MP holds a meeting with the then immigration minister Tony McNulty regarding progress on the further representation. Mr. McNulty confirms verbally that the Home Office has accepted Farhat Khan's submission for consideration as a fresh asylum application.

March 2006

Farhat Khan is invited to speak at an event, 'Asylum-seeking women speak out' organised by Refuge without Borders. It takes place at Portcullis House in Westminster, where MPs have their offices and hold meetings. The event is chaired by Dianne Abbot MP; Farhat's MP attends to show his public support for her asylum application.

May 2006

Graham Stringer receives a letter from Tony McNulty informing that Farhat Khan's case has been forwarded to the relevant case working unit for an asylum interview "to be booked as priority." The family has still not received a written confirmation from the Home Office regarding their fresh asylum application.

Farhat Khan is invited to speak at the ICA, London at an event organised by Women for Refugee Women, for women playing lead roles in media, law and politics. She talks about why she fled Pakistan and the way she and her children have been treated while going through the asylum system in the UK.

June 2006

A NASS outreach team visits Farhat Khan and her children at their home and discusses the family's asylum application in detail. The team are not immigration law specialists but advise Farhat that domestic violence cannot be grounds for asylum, that she will not have the right to ask for a judicial review in the event that her fresh asylum application is refused, and that unless the family agrees to voluntary removal they will be liable to a raid by immigration authorities that could lead to detention and subsequent deportation. Farhat informs them about the fresh asylum application but the team denies any knowledge of the application. After their departure Farhat finds a briefing paper by the Home Office in Liverpool for the NASS team that has been mistakenly left behind. The paper clearly states that a fresh asylum case has been submitted and that Tony McNulty has agreed to "treat the information submitted as a fresh asylum application". Farhat's solicitor makes a complaint to the NASS regional office. The office responds by saying that "It would appear that you have submitted a fresh asylum application but that there is no trace of us receiving it" and that Farhat Khan had discussed her asylum matter with the NASS team of her "own free will."

July 2006

The Joint Council for the Welfare of Immigrants (JCWI) invite Farhat Khan to speak about her experiences as an asylum seeker at the launch of their report 'Recognising Rights, Recognising Political Realities - The Case for Regularisation of Irregular Immigrants' at the House of Commons.

September 2006

Home Office refuses Farhat Khan's application for permission to work on the basis that her asylum application has been refused and all appeal rights exhausted. The letter makes no reference to the fresh asylum application.

December 2006

Farhat Khan receives an invitation from the Prime Minister and Cherie Booth to attend a reception at 10 Downing Street, "in recognition of services to the voluntary sector". Farhat Khan senses that the Prime Minister has been briefed to avoid talking to her; she takes the opportunity anyway to personally thank him for the invitation as "it is not every day that a failed asylum seeker gets invited to Downing Street." The Prime Minister looks taken aback but responds by telling her that he has heard about her, and wishes her and her family "the best of luck."

The media gives detailed coverage, once again highlighting the fact that one hand of the establishment, Downing Street, does not know what another, the Home Office, is doing.

Two days after the reception Farhat Khan attends a four-hour substantive interview at the Home Office, Liverpool, regarding her fresh asylum application.

The Home Office grants permission to work to Farhat Khan after the threat of a judicial review by her solicitor. She decides to continue working full-time as a volunteer at the Cheetham Hill Advice Centre and WAST.

March 2007

Farhat Khan is invited to speak at a meeting organised by Women for Refugee Women at Garden Court Chambers, London. The purpose of the meeting is to bring together organisations working for asylum seekers and the media. Farhat talks about the support offered by WAST to asylum-seeking women.

May 2007

Graham Stringer meets Home Office immigration minister Liam Byrne regarding progress on the fresh asylum application. Byrne agrees to instruct the Casework Directorate to make a decision on the case within a few weeks.

Farhat Khan is invited to speak at a meeting organised by Women for Refugee Women with members of the Parliamentary Labour Party's Women's Committee. The meeting is attended by a number of members from both the houses of parliament who are shocked to hear about the gender discrimination in the asylum system.

June 2007

Farhat Khan gets news from the Home Office announcing the granting of full refugee status her and her three children. The news is given by Farhat's solicitor Gary McIndoe who has been told about the decision in a phone call from the Home Office, Liverpool. The family have been granted five years limited leave to remain in the UK. Farhat Khan collapses in tears on hearing news that she has waited for desperately during every waking moment of the last heartbreakingly long and difficult years. She weeps with mixed feelings - joy and relief at finally having the Home Office accept the truth of her asylum claim, and sadness for the seven lost years of her and her children's lives. Farhat Khan's children are now fifteen, forteen and thirteen years old.

August 2007

NASS informs Farhat Khan that she has to vacate the council house she has been living in for seven years as she is no longer entitled to NASS support. The family is asked to report to the homeless unit at the town hall. Farhat challenges this decision through a housing solicitor as her three children attend the local high school and she works in the local advice centre. The city council accept her right to continue staying in the house on the grounds of having a 'local connection'.

September 2007

Farhat Khan starts paid work at the Cheetham Hill Advice Centre. Additionally she starts work as a part-time tutor as part of a team teaching the post-graduate Certificate of Community Development Workers (BME) at Salford University.

October 2007

Farhat Khan is featured on BBC Radio 4's The Choice, a series of interviews with people who had to make difficult decisions. The interview focuses on her decision to leave Pakistan, her reasons for doing so and how it has affected her later life.

February 2008

Farhat Khan starts work as a lecturer in Community Development Work (BME Mental Health) at Salford University.

July 2012

Farhat Khan and her three children's limited leave to remain will expire. They will have their asylum applications actively reviewed and, if successful, will be allowed to apply for indefinite leave to remain in the UK. Farhat Khan's three children, who were six, seven and nine years when they applied for asylum, will then be 18, 19 and 21 years of age.

USEFUL CONTACTS

Further reading and information on the issue of women and asylum.

INTERNATIONAL

Amnesty International
www.amnesty.org.uk
Protecting individuals wherever justice, fairness, freedom and truth are denied.

Human Rights Watch
www.hrw.org
Protecting the human rights of people around the world.

UNHCR United Nations Refuge Agency
www.unhcr.org
Co-ordinates international action to protect refugees and resolve refugee problems.

CEDAW
www.un.org/womenwatch/daw/cedaw
Convention on the elimination of all forms of discrimination against women.

European Council on Refugees and Exiles
www.ecre.org
An umbrella organization of 68 refugee-assisting member agencies in 25 countries working towards fair and humane policies on asylum.

Office of the High Commissioner for Human Rights
www.unhchr.ch/html/menu2/7/b/women
The United Nations Special Rapporteur on violence against women.

NATIONAL

Asylum Aid Refugee Women's Resource project
www.asylumaid.org.uk
Aims to enable women seeking asylum in the UK to obtain protection and security, maintain their dignity and to be treated with respect during the asylum process.

Women For Refuge Women
www.refugeewomen.com
Promoting the rights of women seeking asylum in the UK.

Black Women's Action Project and Women Against Rape
www.womenagainstrape.org
Offering counselling, support and advice to black women and other women of colour, immigrant and refugee women, who have suffered rape, sexual assault or other violence.

Bail for Immigration Detainees
www.biduk.org
Challenges immigration detention in the UK. Works with asylum seekers and migrants, in removal centres and prisons, to secure their release from detention.

Southall Black Sisters
www.southallblacksisters.org.uk
Aims to meet the needs of black (including Asian) women and to highlight and challenge violence against women.

Rights of Women
www.rightsofwomen.org.uk
Working to attain justice and equality by informing, educating and empowering women on their legal rights.

Committee to Defend Asylum Seekers
www.defend-asylum.org
Opposing government attacks and fighting for the rights of asylum seekers in the UK.

National Coalition Of Anti-Deportation Campaigns
www.ncadc.org.uk
Brings together families and individuals fighting deportation.

Medical Foundation for the Care of Victims of Torture
www.torturecare.org.uk
Provides care and rehabilitation to survivors of torture and other forms of organized violence.

Refuge Action
www.refugee-action.org.uk
Works with refugees to help them build new lives in the UK.

Refuge Council
www.refugeecouncil.org.uk
Providing advice to asylum seekers and refugees and supporting other organisations.

Joint Council for the Welfare of Immigrants

www.jcwi.org.uk

Campaigning for justice and combating racism in immigration and asylum law and policy.

Refugee Legal Centre

www.refugee-legal-centre.org.uk

Legal advice and representation for asylum seekers in the UK.

MANCHESTER

South Manchester Law Centre

www.smlc.org.uk

Specialist legal casework in employment, housing, welfare rights, immigration and women's rights.

George House Trust

www.ght.org.uk

Supports and campaign for the best quality of life for all people living with HIV.

Boaz Trust

www.boaztrust.org.uk

Working with destitute asylum seekers in Greater Manchester.

Manchester Refuge Network (MRSN)

www.mrsn.org.uk

MRSN is a refugee-led charity working to build strong and independent refugee organizations.

Greater Manchester Immigration Aid Unit

www.gmiau.org

Provides legal advice and representation to asylum seekers and others affected by imigration legislation.